CANADIAN WARTIME PRISON ESCAPES

Courage & Daring Behind Enemy Lines

Peter C. Conrad

FOLK LORE PUBLISHING

The Publisher: Folklore Publishing
Website: www.folklorepublishing.com

Library and Archives Canada Cataloguing in Publication

Conrad, Peter C. (Peter Christopher)
    Canadian wartime prison escapes : Courage & daring behind
    enemy lines / Peter C. Conrad.

Includes bibliographical references.
ISBN 13: 978-1-894864-64-0
ISBN 10: 1-894864-64-6

    1. Escapes—Canada—History—20th century. 2. Prisoner-of-war escapes—Canada—History—20th century. 3. Escaped prisoners of war—France—Biography. 4. World War, 1914-1918—Canada—Biography. 5. World War, 1939-1945—Canada—Biography. I. Title.

D805.A2C65 2007   940.54'72092271   C2007-900971-9

Project Director: Faye Boer
Project Editor: Lee Craig
Cover: Photograph by K. Hyde from *In Enemy Hands: Canadian Prisoners of War 1939–45* by Daniel G. Dancocks, 1983, Hurtig Publishers.

We acknowledge the support of the Alberta Foundation for the Arts for our publishing program.

We acknowledge the financial support of the Government of Canada through the Book Publishing Industry Development Program (BPIDP) for our publishing activities.

  Canadian Heritage   Patrimoine canadien

Contents

INTRODUCTION 6

CHAPTER 1: Escaping During World War I. 8

CHAPTER 2: Escaping the Japanese 34

CHAPTER 3: Canadians and MI9 47

CHAPTER 4: Escaping Dieppe. 64

CHAPTER 5: Canadians Return to Occupied France. . 86

CHAPTER 6: Shot Down and Escaped 125

CHAPTER 7: The Canadian Spy Who Escaped 169

CHAPTER 8: Escaping Italian Camps 181

CHAPTER 9: Escaping Eastern Camps. 202

CHAPTER 10: Escaping Stalag Luft III. 208

CHAPTER 11: Those Who Made It Home 241

NOTES ON SOURCES 245

Dedication

This book is dedicated to all those brave men and women who have served Canada at times of war.

Acknowledgements

I would like to give a special thank you to Lee Craig, whose professional editing helped create this polished writing. Faye Boer, the publisher of Folklore Publishing, provided enthusiastic support that assisted me in completing this book. I would like to thank my wife, Simone, for the encouragement and editing she gave me during the first phase of writing this book.

Introduction

These stories were written with extensive research into their subject. They are based on the facts of their events but are presented with an eye to good storytelling. The dialogue, thoughts and emotions of the characters are the writer's inventions since it is impossible to know the feelings of people at the time or the words exchanged. I was fascinated by these episodes of the courageous men who served Canada in war and were either captured by the enemy and escaped or made their way back after getting caught behind enemy lines.

Many people see a clear distinction between the soldiers or airmen who were captured, escaped and then made their way to the Allied lines and those who found themselves behind enemy lines and evaded capture to return to safety. Those men who escaped from prison camps and returned to Allied territory have been called "escapees." Servicemen who found themselves behind enemy lines and evaded capture to return home have been called "evaders." In this book the general term of escapee is applied to both. Doing so is a reflection of the fact that both the escapees and the evaders were in the same situation. Regardless of whether the escapee first escaped from a prisoner of war camp or was behind enemy lines, both were escaping occupied countries where those who helped them faced summary executions. The servicemen who were making their way out of occupied countries had to depend on the good will of the local people, blend into the population and determinedly follow a plan to escape. The final goal remained the same for those who were behind enemy lines: escape from the threat of capture to return home.

This book has a careful selection of stories about the courageous servicemen who made their way to the freedom of the Allied lines during the world wars. It also tells the stories of the extraordinary acts of bravery of the civilians, women and men, in the occupied countries during the world wars. This book is a tribute to the acts of courage and bravery that contributed to the Allied victories.

CHAPTER ONE

Escaping During World War I

DURING WORLD WAR I (1914–19), THERE WAS A VERY DIFFERENT sentiment among Canadians about prisoners of war than during World War II. Many people did not want to hear the stories of the men who suffered from the cold or heat, starvation, beatings and neglect behind the barbed wire. Some people believed that prisoners of war had brought their plight in the camps upon themselves. Heroic soldiers were supposed to die or fight to their deaths before accepting defeat and capture. The stories of the men who were prisoners of the enemy during World War I were ignored as were their experiences of war—many believed their chronicles would taint the victory of the Allies.

Men who escaped prison camps were thought to be spies for the enemy. Escaping was not considered a widely accepted duty during World War I as it was during World War II. Most captured soldiers believed that the war was over for them and that they would have to spend the rest of the war in a camp.

The efforts of those men who successfully escaped were astounding, given the attitudes that existed. There were many significant obstacles for those who escaped from prisoner of war camps in Germany during World War I, but there were also opportunities to escape that did not exist in World War II. For example, officers were often allowed to leave the prison camps in Germany to walk where they wished. They were expected to return on their honour. Both the Germans, and even many Allies, would have been horrified by the dishonour of officers who did not return.

During both world wars, becoming a prisoner of war did not mean you were no longer on duty as service personnel. Men who were in prisoner of war camps were expected to give their military host the same respect for rank as they would their own officers. For example, a Canadian soldier was expected to salute a German officer as he would salute a British or Canadian officer. This kind of discipline was thought to be the best way to deal with the routines, rigours and boredom that characterized prison camps.

Other prisoners who were not officers were allowed to volunteer for work in local factories and on the nearby farms. There was no expectation that officers or any other rank of soldier would simply walk away to trek across the country and find their way back to their own side. Many soldiers, after fighting in the trenches, risking death and struggling continuously against the cold, mud and gas, did not want to risk escaping to return to it. Readers might think that soldiers who escaped would make a more significant contribution on the front lines; they were outraged by the Kaiser's war and the German brutality they experienced in work camps or during punishments for infractions, including attempted escapes. However, prisoners who successfully escaped returned to the Canadian Armed Forces as instructors or trainers. Escapees who arrived in a neutral country such as Holland before being transferred back to the Allies had to sign a formal agreement not to return to combat. These agreements were in place to protect the neutrality of the country that was assisting the escapees return home. Still other escapees were sent back to Canada because the authorities were suspicious of them.

One of the first Canadians to successfully escape, and the only Canadian officer to escape, was Major Peter Anderson, a Danish-Canadian. As soon as he was captured at the end of April 1915, Anderson decided he would escape. He started to carry out his plan by avoiding having his picture taken shortly after his capture. He was also careful to avoid the attention of his captors as he planned his escape.

Peter Anderson was taken to the new cavalry barracks just constructed at Bischofswerda in the German state of Saxony. Anderson sought out and found a British officer from the Cameron Highlanders, Lord James Murray, who was willing to teach him German. Anderson's plan was based on finding his way to Switzerland where he had friends. Peter thought his plan would take three months to complete, but it stretched out for five months. He intended to use his newly learned German language skills to make his way to Denmark.

To carry out his plan, he used his privileges as an officer to walk to a local village and shop for the articles he needed for his escape. Peter found a sturdy pair of boots, a pipe, a knapsack, additional socks and a rubber cushion that he expected would be useful if he had to cross a river. In the village shops, Anderson was able to buy a black oilskin coat and woolen gloves. To complete his disguise, Peter found a checked cap that was popular with tourists at the time.

Anderson began his escape run on September 28, 1915, right before the harvest, so that he could use the standing crops in the countryside to hide. If he left too late in the year, after harvest, the cold and wet conditions would hinder his escape. Anderson was helped to escape through a stable at the prison and then over a 13-foot-high fence by Lieutenant Edward Bellow, who had been with the 7th Battalion, and Lieutenant Frank Smith, who had been with the 15th Battalion.

Rain poured down as Anderson escaped from the camp. Anderson first went south with the intention of appearing to head for Switzerland, but after two hours he changed his direction. Soon, it became clear that the rain was a blessing. He had noticed that men were tracking him with dogs. The rain had washed out his scent.

Once at Guben, Peter took the next step in his plan. He identified himself as a Swedish-American carpenter named Peter Jansson who was grief-stricken because his German friend, Hans Schmidt, had just died for the Fatherland. With such a public display of emotion, no one asked him for his papers as he boarded a train that took him near the Danish border, where he quietly exited the train when it stopped. Peter noticed that the border sentry was drunk and asleep, and he was able to slip across to his old homeland.

Peter Anderson arrived in London on October 2, 1915, and he received a cool reception. He was among the first escapees to arrive, but he was also a Danish-Canadian with a German accent. Peter was the highest-ranking serviceman to successfully make his way back. The fact that he was 47 years old added to the suspicion he faced. Many people believed he was a German agent, but they were unable to prove anything. Peter Anderson was given staff and training duties at Shorncliffe, an army garrison that was west of Folkestone in the Kent district in England.

Both John Vaughan and Jack Hollett of the Canadian Mounted Rifles were captured at Mont Sorrel, a wooded area that rose up to the east of

Ypres, France. Mont Sorrel was strategically advan-
tageous—those who held the area could look out
over the lower land to the west and Ypres itself.
The two soldiers worked together on their plan to
escape when they were sent to a chemical factory
at Duisburg to work. Vaughan had a lucky break
when he found a map, which he immediately
stole. To protect himself from harsh punishment,
usually a beating and solitary confinement, he
buried it until they were ready to escape.

Vaughan's luck continued. He was able to use
some of his winnings from a card game to buy
a compass from a German. He had enough money
left over to buy the caps and clothes he and Hollett
needed to look like Belgian workers during their
trek to Holland, their intended destination.

The two were ready to escape on November 26,
1916. The escape plan called for their fellow prisoners to make a great deal of noise over a card
game so that Vaughan and Hollett could push
themselves through a partition at the camp that
separated the prisoners from the Belgian workers.
Once on the other side, the Belgian workers helped
the two to leave their building. The Belgian workers' building was attached to the prison, but there
was no security around it. The two escapees, like
the Belgian workers, could simply walk out the
door to freedom.

Shortly after their escape, the pair walked right
into a German officer on the street. The two

stepped back and bowed to the officer, who passed by without a second look. Vaughan and Hollett found a boat and made their way west on the Rhine River. At one point, they passed a German sentry and were ignored as they greeted him with a *Guten morgen*.

As they neared their destination, the Dutch border, a child noticed them and called out. The two ran for a nearby forest where they hid for two days. Vaughan and Hollett then tried to cross the Dutch border, but they noticed a German sentry nearby and quickly ran back to the woods to wait for nighttime to provide the cover they needed for another attempt. On the night of November 30, 1916, between 2:00 AM and 3:00 AM, Vaughan and Hollett crawled in the cold dark and mist toward the sentry line where they heard a guard cough. They stopped and waited until the guard walked away into the darkness. Over the cold, wet ground, the two crawled quickly toward the border. They continued on in the dark, sure that they were in Holland. They took no risks, lying low and remaining hidden by a railroad until daybreak.

Shortly after the sun rose, Vaughan and Hollett watched a Dutch railroad work crew arrive for the day's work. The two Canadians felt safe and came out of hiding and received a warm welcome. They were given food, baths and medical help. After a week, they made their way back to England.

During World War I, prisoners tried to dig tunnels to allow escapees a route out of the camps without the risk of being shot. The most famous tunnel escape dug during World War I was at the prison camp at Holzminden.

At the Holzminden prison camp, Commandant Niemeyer, nicknamed "Milwaukee Bill," was disliked by most prisoners. The prisoners had no trouble finding participants to dig the tunnel, which was planned and organized by Lieutenant J.G. Colquhoun, an officer with the Princess Patricia's Canadian Light Infantry.

The entrance to the tunnel was under a staircase. The men who were digging the tunnel only had a compass to guide them. Unfortunately, the compass was often not accurate when used underground, and the tunnel curved for over 180 feet. It also had to curve around rock that had been a part of a streambed.

As the tunnel became longer, a lack of fresh air became a problem for the diggers. A bellows was made from a prisoner's leather flight jacket. To avoid cave-ins, which were always a problem, supports for the tunnel had to be constructed from boards taken from the beds.

The men building the tunnel realized they needed another method other than using a compass underground to dig the tunnel in a straight line and to check how far it had progressed. The men decided to attach a small rag to a wire and push it up to ground level. As the flag pushed out of the ground, a prisoner would be on the upper floor of the building watching. Once the observer saw the flag he reported the progress and sent a message. The flag was quickly retracted.

Work progressed slowly as workers crawled to the front of the digging and used table knives and a chisel to dig and then load the sand and dirt into small containers. These full containers had to be carried out and the contents disposed of surreptitiously. The workers often wore few clothes because it was difficult to clean them and the tunnel was hot and damp.

The tunnel quickly became a place for rats. Many of the workers met them as they made their way in, seeing the glint of their eyes. They often heard the rats as they moved, and it was common to feel vermin scurrying across their backs as they crawled to the digging site. The dirty rat-infested conditions of the trenches at the front had already hardened many of the men to the rats in the tunnel.

The slow steady work on the tunnel took nine months to complete. There were many Appelle— roll calls—that demanded the workers be quickly pulled from the tunnels, dressed and hurried to the surface.

When the work was completed on the tunnel, 29 men pushed their bundles through and escaped on the night of July 23, 1918. The long, curving, tight tunnel took the escapees out of the prison camp into a bean patch near a field of rye. Six more officers had pushed their way into the tunnel when it started to collapse. These six needed help in pulling themselves out because each had large bundles of civilian clothes with them.

The tunnel was a great success. Ten of the men who crawled out from under the prison fences of Holzminden made it across the Dutch border while another 19 were recaptured. When Commandant Niemeyer realized the magnitude of the escape, he was furious. He was so outraged that he sent a guard into the building the prisoners were in to shoot someone. One prisoner was on the stairs as the guard fired his rifle. The bullet missed the man and crashed through a window.

There were many prisoners during World War I who successfully escaped, but only after several attempts. One of these was Mervyn Simmons from British Columbia. To ensure he would be able to escape if captured, he sewed a small compass into his uniform.

After Simmons arrived at the Giessen prisoner of war camp, he approached Frank Bromley, who was also from British Columbia and had been a student at Heidelberg. Bromley was able to provide information about Germany. As Simmons prepared his escape plan, he found out which men were suspected of being German double agents and avoided them.

Simmons' careful activities and low profile in the prison paid off when he got a chance to become an agricultural worker. Bromley and Simmons were sent to a farm near Rossbach to work with a kind, easygoing farmer. The pleasant conditions did not make Simmons or Bromley change their minds; they continued to make plans to escape.

On the early morning of October 3, 1915, Simmons and Bromley began their run for the Swiss border. They were determined to succeed even though it was clear that the coming winter with its cold and wet weather would make the trek difficult. The two struggled against the elements with little help. After two weeks on the land, a child spotted them, and a nearby platoon of German trainees intercepted the men. A German general questioned them, and the two were marched back to Giessen. The compass was taken away, and the escapees suffered beatings and solitary confinement for their escape effort. Prisoners who faced such sanctions were also denied their mail and Red Cross parcels. The rations in the German prisoner of war camps were meagre, and the Red Cross parcels made a great difference to the prisoners' comfort.

In January 1916, Simmons and Bromley partnered with Corporal Ted Edwards, who had been with the Princess Patricia's Canadian Light Infantry. Even after suffering punishment and starvation rations for months, Simmons and Bromley continued to plan their next escape. Simmons received a parcel from his brother and found a compass in a container of cream cheese. The two were also able to get their hands on a tattered map of Germany.

The three men were moved to Vehnenmoor prison camp, where Edwards cut the barbwire of the camp's fence, and the men made a run for freedom. Luck did not hold for Bromley as his leg gave out, and the other two were forced to move on without him. Simmons and Edwards made it to the River Ems and found themselves surrounded by German patrols and sentries. They tried to cross the bridge, but their hunger and ragged clothes alerted the Germans, and they were captured.

The two were marched back to Vehnenmoor by an elderly Landstürmer, or German infantryman, past hostile villagers who cursed and spat on them. They were confined to cells for 11 days and fed thin soup and black bread. But the men had a reprieve from one of their German guards. The guard brought the two a pot of soup and white bread to share.

Finally, a court marshal was organized. Both Simmons and Edwards were convicted and sentenced to 30 days of "strenger arrest," which meant they were to receive a severe punishment. Their sentences were to be carried out at the Oldenburg fortress. The two men found themselves imprisoned at Oldenburg with German non-commissioned officers (NCO) and soldiers who were also sentenced to the same punishment.

The two Canadians found themselves in small, dark, steel-walled cells without heat and with very high ceilings. The first part of the punishment usually took from 14 to 30 days. The prisoners were locked into the cells for three days and given only a jug of water and a piece of bread. The cells were kept darkened, and each day the prisoners had 10 minutes to go to the lavatory and clean their cells as well as they could. The routine changed on the fourth day, when the light was turned on and they were given a bowel of soup. Then the routine would be the same as for the first three days.

The conditions for Simmons got worse when the guards took away his overcoat. The starvation diet was making him too weak to walk without feeling extremely exhausted. He began to feel sick continuously, which came to a climax on a soup day when the guards forgot to bring his food. He fell to the floor with an intense grip of hunger pain that brought on a cold sweat. Simmons believed he would die during the night. But he survived the first phase of the punishment.

Simmons and Edwards were transferred to the Parnewinkel work camp, joining between 400 and 500 Russians, about 80 French and 11 British. The two Canadians were filthy and emaciated. The British prisoners shared with them what they could

from their Red Cross parcels. A vengeful commandant and abusive guards commanded the harsh
camp. While the Russians worked on the farms
around the prison, the British cleaned latrines.

Simmons was even more driven by his experiences to escape. He was not sure if he would sur-
vive in the German prisoner of war camps now
that he was singled out as a troublemaker. He had
learned from his past attempts, and he would not
fail on his third effort. Simmons and Edwards
gathered their strength for a third attempt once
their punishment was over.

Both men wasted no time in preparing their
next escape attempt. With increased determination, they agreed they would take no chances as
they made their way to freedom—they would trust
no one in Germany, and they would take every
precaution along the way. They started collecting
what they would need to make their trip, starting
with a compass and maps. At Vehnemoor, Edwards
had bought a map of Germany that was detailed
and included every railroad and branch line, even
those that ended without linking to any other rail
line. Having this level of detail was particularly
useful because the two knew that the end points
of the railroad lines in northern Germany indicated unpopulated areas where the land was infer-
tile and of little economic interest. Simmons had
used other maps to draw his own, and when he
saw Edward's map, he added the railroad lines so
they had two copies of the same map.

Simmons had a small watertight tin that he'd received in a Red Cross parcel where he stored some matches. Edwards also had a magnifying glass they planned to use to light their pipes and start fires in order to save their matches.

The men first planned to cut the wire of the fence around the camp to escape, but doing so wasn't possible after three Russians escaped that way in the spring of 1916. The Germans had increased surveillance on the fence to prevent anyone approaching it. Simmons and Edwards agreed the best approach was to volunteer for work on a nearby farm, which was not easy because they were considered to be Englishmen and more likely to cause trouble in work parties, unlike the Russians. The two men knew that they had a better chance of getting on to a work party if they appeared to be morose, depressed and listless, like men who had given up all hope. Every time the German guards were around, they displayed their hopeless feelings.

After a time, their acting worked. The Germans didn't expect any more trouble from Simons and Edwards. Both appeared to be broken. They were allowed on the work crews. Aware that the work parties provided opportunities for escape, the commandant of the prisoner of war camp began having prisoners searched often and at unexpected times. Simmons and Bromley realized that they would not be able to leave with all the supplies they had gathered for their escape. They reduced what they would take to only a few things: compass, razor, tin box of matches, soap, magnifying glass, maps, comb, toothbrushes, tobacco, pipes, safety pins, pocketknife and some string. Many of the items were carefully concealed in their clothes. The two had hoped to carry a full supply of food as well, but that was impossible. The day before they made their escape, they ate from their supplies and gave the rest to their fellow prisoners as gifts.

They continued to appear dejected and defeated while they were in the prison camp and worked hard when they were allowed to participate in workdays outside the camp. The entire work gang had only one guard, who had become certain that the prisoners had no chance of escape.

On one Saturday morning roll call, there was a request for workers to go to a farm four miles away to weed a field of turnips. While the men ate their supper in the farmhouse kitchen and the guard visited with the farm family elsewhere, Simmons and Edwards slipped out the back door into the night. It was much darker than usual. Heavy, dark clouds had formed, blocking any light from the moon. The two hurried away, unnoticed, walking right by the farmer's daughter, who was busy feeding the pigs. They walked quickly along the lane in front of the farmhouse to the village beyond. They both knew that the guard wouldn't be able to pursue them. He had to stay at the farmhouse to supervise the rest of the men. The only fear the two had was that the guard would hurry after them and shoot one of them as they fled. They knew that they wouldn't have to fear the guard when they could take cover in a wooded area on the other side of the village. At that moment, it began to rain. Even though they didn't like being cold and wet, Simmons and Edwards also knew that a search party was less likely to pursue them in the dark forest at night.

The two checked their compass and hurried through the heavy rain south to Bremen. They travelled around the town in a wide circle to avoid being seen. They wanted to go west to Holland, but the trek would bring them close to densely populated areas, which were far too dangerous. They continued along in the more unpopulated forested areas. At one point, they had to wade through a fast-flowing stream. They passed through a field of turnips, and because they had no food, they quickly dug up as many as they could before hurrying to take cover in a wooded area for the day. Wet and tired, Simmons and Edwards waited in the forest and did not reveal themselves even when a dog from a nearby farm approached and barked at them.

The men continued along in the unpopulated areas that were marked by marshes and peat bogs. By avoiding populated areas, they were safe from discovery, but they were also faced with a lack of food. They often had to approach farms in order to find food.

On the night of August 23, 1916, the two saw a distant glow from the lights of Bremen. As they made their way south in an effort to go around the city to the south and east, they had to cross a river. They accepted that they would have to swim. They had agreed that they would not attempt to cross any bridges because they were likely to be guarded. Simmons took off his clothes, placed them in a bundle and swam across first. He then returned to help Edwards, who was already trying to swim across on his back holding his clothes high, but he lost the bundle. Simmons retrieved it and brought it to the far shore. They got dressed, but Edwards' clothing was especially soaked from being dropped in the water.

The two were exhausted, wet and cold when they found a place in a wooded area to rest during the day. They had not eaten and had a restless day waiting for the darkness of the night to start moving again. That night they found a cow along the way and milked it, filling the pail they were using for their matches. They drank their fill and were feeling much better when they came across a railroad. They located it on their map and knew exactly where they were. Soon, they came to the Weser River and decided to hide in the willows along the bank for the day. They hurried back to a field nearby to gather straw to make warm a bed for the day.

When darkness fell, they searched for a boat to cross the river. They found one before too long and

were on the other side of the river and on their
way again. Simmons' and Edwards' good luck continued. Again they found several cows and drank
their fill of milk. They also found apples, and when
day broke, they found a shrub that had a closed-in
area underneath. They crawled inside for the day.
Later, a dog found them and barked, but the man
walking it called it away. Afterwards, a group of
children played a ball game close to their hiding
place.

The two continued their journey westward that
night and hid in a forest during the next day. It
began to rain again. They continued in the forest
the next night, but they found themselves con-
fused many times because they came across many
roads. Simmons and Edwards had to stop a lot to
consult their compass, but that consumed too
many matches. The cold, hunger and exhaustion
made them feel more depressed than at any other
time during their journey. They lost their sense of
caution and decided to pursue food aggressively
the next night. As they walked, they saw a group
of cows in a shed and wasted no time going right
inside. As they milked and drank, they listened to
a heavy downpour. They stayed dry and warm in
the shed. As morning approached, they hurried
along their way and found a tight clump of evergreens to crawl under and sleep. Even through
they couldn't stand up, it was a good hiding place.

The next night the two escapees came to the
Hunte River. They decided that they were not

going to take the same risks they had in earlier crossings with their clothes. They decided to return to a farm nearby where they saw a large wooden gate. The two removed the gate and carried it to the bank of the river. They placed their clothes on it, and Simmons swam ahead pulling the floating gate while Edwards swam behind pushing it. They arrived on the opposite side of the river with dry clothes.

After hiding three days, they set out towards the west, gathering food each night. On September 3, they were able to make their first fire in a wooded area because the early morning mists hid the smoke. The men placed over two dozen potatoes they had found in nearby fields on the fire to cook. They removed the charred peel and filled their bellies, keeping the rest for the following days. As evening approached, the two came out of their hiding place and went to a trail to locate where they were before night fell. Suddenly, an elderly man appeared on the trail with a gun and a dog. Simmons and Edwards quickly stepped off the path and motioned for the man to pass. He looked at them, said good evening, passed by and continued on his way. No search party appeared as they hurried away.

Simmons and Edwards passed a settlement made up of new buildings. That night, as they walked, they found that many of the houses along the road had full milk tins at the roadside for early morning pick up. When they opened the tins, they found that the cream had risen to the top, and they had many stops to dip their tin can in to drink the cream. They also found apple trees and filled up their pockets.

The two men followed a road that came to an end where a large pile of peat cut from nearby bogs was stacked for the winter. The night was dark as they continued on their way over other uneven and rough bogs. They felt exhausted and lost their sense of direction, making it necessary to check their compass many times. As the first light of the morning pushed through the darkness, they came to the edge of the bog, where they found a run-down hut in the woods that must have been built for a cow herder. They had just settled in when a woman walked by the hut, looked at them, smiled and shook her head as she waved. She walked on and looked back and shook her head with a smile again. The two men saw a few sacks, which they took and ran for a thick forest nearby. They spent the day trying to sleep, fearful that the woman had reported them and that a search party would appear. Nothing happened. It started to sprinkle as the evening set in, and they continued on their way exhausted and unsure of their own success. The rain cleared off, and they continued until the morning, when they again found a wooded area to sleep.

The night that followed provided some light from the moon, so that the men could more easily make out the ridges and holes of the thick peat bog. They came out of the bog near a village, and they saw the massive searchlights at Oldenburg, where they had faced such cruel punishment for attempting to escape previously. They were cautious as they hurried on to the next village. They searched for apples but found that the trees had been picked bare. As they walked through the village, a door suddenly opened and two German soldiers stepped out. The escapees dropped to the ground and quickly threw the sacks they had been carrying over themselves and lay still in the dark. They listened breathlessly as the two soldiers laughed and talked and made their way up the street. Simmons and Edwards were so frightened that they didn't bother looking for food anymore. They hurried on their way until they found a thick stand of evergreens that they could hide in for the day.

The next night, they tried to avoid all villages, but they were so closely placed together that no matter how hard they tried, they found themselves in yet another village. They hurried westward as fast as they could until they found another wooded area, where they started a fire and roasted potatoes. Unfortunately, morning came so quickly they had to extinguish it. They lay quietly as they saw people in all directions working in fields and shepherding flocks with dogs. Both the shepherd and an elderly man in a field saw them, but they went on with their work. The escapees felt nervous and edgy as the day wore on, fearful that they would be captured only miles from freedom. Edwards found a heavy stick he intended to use as a club if he had to fight anyone. They saw a thicker wood close by and quickly moved to it.

As the evening brought the fading light of the day, the two were anxious to continue. After dark, they quickly came to a railroad that the map indicated ran parallel to the Ems River. It was about 3:00 AM when they reached the river, which appeared large and difficult to cross. They went back to a potato field and filled a sack before returning to the bank for the day. They set a fire and roasted potatoes. They stayed on the bank during the day watching people, steam boats and canal boats pass close to their hiding place.

After dark, they moved to the bank and noticed a fence that had a gate to a pasture. Again they pulled the gate off to use as a floating device for the pack with their clothes and easily made the swim across the river. After another hour of walking, they came to a canal that they easily swam across. They were now very close to the border, so both men were cautious. They were certain they would run into German patrols. They felt an urgency to hurry to the trees that stood on the other side of a road, but they saw a hole being dug. They took their clothes and slipped into the hole to dress. Seconds later, they heard and saw a German patrol walk by. Once the guards had passed, they quietly finished dressing and then rushed out of the hole and across the road.

Simmons and Edwards knew that they were at the border, and there was a chance of meeting more German patrols.

"We're close to freedom," whispered Edwards.

"But we could run into the Germans here," said Simmons.

"We need a plan," said Edwards.

"What?" asked Simmons. "We just keep going."

"If they come after us," said Edwards, "we should just run like hell."

"Don't give up," said Simmons.

"At least one of us should make it."

"All right," said Simmons.

The two came to a marsh that they could see in the moonlight. It lay flat and stretched out into the distance. When they stepped on it they realized that it was a quaking bog or a hidden lake with a matted surface that would sink if you stood a moment too long. They barely spoke as they began to run across it, the surface dropping to cover their feet with water as they went. Fear gave them the speed they needed to rush across the expanse until they made it to the other side. They stopped when they saw a pile of cut peat, indicating that they were on solid ground.

After a short rest, they were on the way again. They reached another canal in minutes. Excitement swept over Simmons because he was sure they were in Holland. This canal was not on any of the maps of Germany he had copied out.

They swam across the canal and found a thicket to stay in the next day. They wanted to be certain they were in Holland before showing themselves. They watched as a team of horses ploughed a field. Because there were few horses in Germany, they took the horses as another sign that they were in Holland. Looking at the larger map detailing the railroads, the two men realized that if they came to a light railroad on a dirt grating when they walked west, they were indeed in Holland. Before midnight, the men came across the single line railroad that indicated that they were in Holland.

On the night of September 9 they were free to walk along the roads and across bridges. By morning, they found a burnt-out house to sleep in. The two men were discovered and were soon speaking with the Dutch authorities who first asked them to stay for the duration of the war in Holland and work. Simmons and Edwards insisted that they return to England. They were given papers to sign that barred them from returning to active combat, which was a requirement for all those who escaped from Germany through neutral Holland.

After Simmons gave a full account of his capture and escapes to the British and Canadian authorities, he was sent back to his family in Toronto. In 1918, Nellie McClung wrote the book *Three Times and Out Told by Private Simmons*. It was published by Thomas Allen Publishers of Toronto. The publication of this book showed that the negative attitude towards prisoners of war and escapees was changing for the better.

Ninety-nine Canadian soldiers escaped successfully during the World War I, with Peter Anderson being the only officer to escape the German prisoner of war camps. There have been many accounts of those who attempted to escape, but Lord Beaverbrook had them edited and embellished to assist in war propaganda, tainting these reports.

CHAPTER TWO

Escaping the Japanese

IN ALL THE STORIES OF ESCAPE AND EVASION FROM THE
enemy during World War II, consistent elements
are present. The escapees were determined and
single-minded in their efforts and had clear plans.
The men's ability to blend into the local population
and the untiring assistance of the local people,
regardless of the penalties they would face if discovered, were essential to successful escapes. In
those cases where escapees could not blend into
the local population, they had to journey to freedom in total secrecy, finding hiding places along
the way. In this story, these escape strategies were
tested to the utmost. The Canadian servicemen
who found themselves behind enemy lines in Asia
were unable to blend into the population because
of significant differences in appearance.

During World War II, alliances were not always
as strong as they seemed, and the relationship
between the governments of Siam and Japan was
one such example. The Japanese were confident
that Siam was an ally when Japan's forces occupied Siam during December 1941. The Siamese

government was immediately co-operative, and soon after, on January 25, 1942, it declared war on the Allies. But behind the scenes, Siam was conducting activities that worked against the Japanese. Powerful government ministers began organizing the Siamese Resistance. The Siamese Resistance quickly made contact with the Special Operations Executive (SOE) mission, based in India, through Siamese government channels. SOE was a British covert operations service that provided agents and supplies to sabotage enemy war facilities, manufacturing, transportation and communications. Once contacted, the SOE helped Siam, but the efforts of the SOE were delayed while other intrigues in the Siamese government came to an end.

The SOE supplied the Siamese Resistance using Liberator bombers and Catalina aircraft that had been modified to fly longer ranges. These supply runs typically flew from India. The Resistance effort in northern Siam continued to develop until late in 1944, when large regions came under its control. Resistance members then built landing fields for the SOE aircraft to supplement the drop sites that they initially used. These developments allowed SOE to provide more supplies to the Siamese Resistance, which continued to harass the Japanese in the air and on the ground. Japanese patrols often faced intense opposition from the local population, and many Japanese soldiers were quickly killed and buried.

On one of the SOE missions to Siam to deliver supplies, Flying Officer Harry Smith of the Royal Canadian Air Force (RCAF) had to evade the Japanese. Smith was flying a Liberator that was equipped for long-range flights and had a crew of nine. Smith was flying with No. 358 Squadron out of the Jassore district, which was close to Calcutta. That day's flight was a special duties operation to supply the Siamese Resistance and to drop off four American special operations agents.

The flight had been uneventful. As the sun rose above the horizon, the Liberator was closing in on the drop-off site. But at that moment, nine "Oscar" Japanese fighter planes attacked. Three of the Liberator's crewmen were killed, and the Liberator caught fire. Smith was faced with a crisis when all four engines effectively shut down. He had to land the bomber and attempt to save as many lives as he could in the forests below. He ordered the crew to prepare for a crash moments before the aircraft descended into the heavy growth. Smith aimed the fuselage of the Liberator at the trees, which stripped the wings off the aircraft as it came down. The body of the plane skidded through the trees and brush for about 300 yards before it came to a stop. The crash-landing killed one crewmember and one special operations agent.

As Harry Smith struggled to get out of his seat, he realized that he had a head injury and that his back and ankle hurt. Smith climbed out of the remains of the Liberator where he met others who had made it out. They were dazed and disoriented. Smith returned to wreckage to free the others who were trapped inside. He found Corporal Napieral-ski, an American who was badly injured, and pulled him from the plane. The other crewmem-bers were working on building a stretcher for Napi-eralski when they heard approaching voices and dogs barking. They were sure that a search party of Japanese was closing in on them. Smith gave the senior American operative the escape kit, his revolver and a heavy knife called a kukri to cut the heavy vegetation of the forest. Smith said he would stay with Napieralski and the rest should attempt to escape.

As the group left, Smith passed out for a moment. When he regained consciousness, he felt a sense of urgency. He stood up and hurried to the remains of the Liberator. Smith destroyed the codebooks and radios and took the dead navigator's escape kit. He then pulled out some parachutes, medical supplies, a survival kit and two rifles. As he emerged from the Liberator, he faced about 100 well-armed natives. As Smith slowly climbed out of the wrecked aircraft, the natives stayed back from the remains of the crashed bomber.

Harry Smith took out a blood chit, which was a flag carried by airmen in case they were shot down and needed to ask people for help in their language. The blood chit had a printed message on it. Smith presented the blood chit, and the natives became much more friendly. Smith was given water to drink and to wash Napieralski's wounds, but soon Napieralski died.

Smith gathered his supplies and was ready to go wherever the natives wanted to take him. After walking about a kilometre through the forest, they came to a village, where Smith was taken to the chief. The chief gave Smith some rice and told him that he had to leave. It was too risky for him to stay. A couple of the men agreed to take Smith to the next village, about 2.5 kilometres away. When Smith arrived, he discovered that the rest of the men from his aircraft were there.

Smith found that the crewmembers had worse injuries than they had first thought. Some of them had severe burns and bullet wounds, and they were not able to move as fast as they had hoped. The group had walked for a while, but they found local people surrounding them. As the wounded men waited in the cover of the forest, Major Gildee, an American operative, approached the natives and found that they were willing to help. The men were guided to the village, where they were told that if they handed over their arms, the people would help them. The crewmembers agreed, so the villagers gave them rice, and they were allowed to stay in the chief's house, where they set to work tearing up the parachutes they had brought so that they could make bandages. They used the bandages plus some antiseptic from their medical supplies to dress their wounds.

The crewmembers stayed in the village for the night, but they were surprised in the morning when they were confronted by a group of Siamese hill police who had heard of their presence. The police also knew that a Japanese patrol would be travelling through the village later that day as a part of the occupying force's routine. An English-speaking member of the police told the aircrew that the police were there to take them where the Japanese would not find them.

The crewmen were not well enough to quickly cover the 4.5 kilometres from the village to the lake, which was deeper in the forest, so the police arranged for them to be given rides on bullock carts. They soon arrived at a hiding place and were told that for their safety they would stay there for the day. Their hosts provided meals of rice and fruit.

As the airmen and the police waited at the lake, an aircraft with Siamese markings arrived. The men from the Liberator watched nervously as the police, including a chief of police from the Nakaun Sawan district, got out of the aircraft. Another group of Siamese police had been sent to where the Liberator had crashed. They had buried the dead at the site and gathered what equipment they could.

The Japanese responded as soon as news of the crash made its way to the officials in the area. They quickly organized about 70 soldiers to sweep through the area to find any survivors. As the Japanese were organizing their search, one of their officers telephoned the police headquarters at Nakaun to speak with the chief of police. The chief's assistant told the Japanese that the chief was out on business. He was actually organizing the escape of the Liberator crew and passengers. With the impending arrival of an aggressive ground search in the area, the chief of police got set to move the men as far away as he could. The airmen were loaded on three bullock carts, and they started on their way. The trek continued non-stop until midnight, when the passengers were given a meal of chicken and rice.

With a new set of three bullock carts and an escort of three men on horses, the crewmen were on their way again. The police worked tirelessly to clean up the racks and remove evidence of the places the airmen might have got off the carts. Others told villagers who saw them pass what they were to say if the Japanese came and asked questions. The police found out that two Japanese soldiers had arrived at a village close to where they had stopped. The Japanese soldiers were immediately shot, and the villagers worked quickly to bury their bodies and remove all evidence that they had been there.

The men continued on their trek until around noon on the third day, when they stopped at another village and received a complete meal. They felt safe enough to stay where they were for

the afternoon and evening and slept until nightfall, when they continued on their way. The fourth
day was difficult because they did not stop. They
had to ration the water and only had a few pine-
apples to share.

Early in the morning, the group arrived in one
of the largest villages along their route. The village
had a trained doctor who was able to provide care
for the wounded. They also enjoyed a full meal
and rested for a while. The police arranged for
a covered cart that was pulled by oxen, so fewer
people would see them on the trek. Once this was
arranged, the airmen were taken to a river where
they got onto two covered boats that were about
30 feet long. The group prepared to leave, but they
had to wait as a storm broke.

In the darkness of night, the escapees were
finally on their way as the oarsmen took them
down the river and onto a lake. Around midnight,
they came to a houseboat occupied by a friendly
Chinese family, who gave the men food and
dressed their wounds again. The crewmen were
invited back for a visit after the war. The police
then arrived to take them onto the next part of
their trek. The chief of police said farewell at this
point because he had to return to his duties, and
other police took the men out on rowboats across
the lake.

The escapees felt apprehensive when they
learned that the police were taking them ashore

where they would be guided across a railway line that was guarded by Japanese soldiers. The men had become comfortable with the way the Siamese were able to keep them at a distance from the Japanese throughout the journey. As they prepared to move on, every man was reminded of where they were and the danger that surrounded them. One at a time, the airmen crept across the railroad tracks and then on to the river beyond where they got into a large police boat that was covered in the middle. The escapees sat closely together under the cover as the boat made its way up the river. With the men hidden, there were no enquiries from the Japanese forces, who were actively guarding the region. The large boat carried a police captain, a lieutenant and six regular police officers. There were also six airmen and three Americans. The crew included a driver, an engineer and a cook, who was the engineer's wife. The group had a long way to go, and they travelled all day. Without stopping, they kept steaming along as night fell.

The journey continued on into the afternoon of the next day, one week since the crash. The boat finally came to a stop at an area around Bangkok. The police had an arrangement for the crewmen to go to one of the local police stations in a covered bus so no one would know who was being brought in. The survivors from the crashed Liberator arrived at a station on the rim of Bangkok, where medical staff changed the dressings on their wounds. The police also gave the men a complete meal and accommodations for the night.

A police officer awakened the leaders of the group, Smith and Major Gildee, early in the morning and asked them to quietly follow. The two men found themselves before a Thai general who was one of the top leaders of the Siamese Resistance. He was extremely anti-Japanese. Despite his feelings about the occupation, he was worried that the Japanese were asking too many questions. It was clear to the Japanese officers that the crewman had local help to avoid the occupying forces. Fearing for the Resistance movement and the lives of the Liberator crew and the people who had helped them, the Resistance leaders decided to tell the Japanese that the Liberator had nine crewmen aboard and that five had died and were buried. Four others would have to be placed in a Siamese prison with a full report given to the occupying powers. Smith and Gildee had to choose which men would be imprisoned. The general made it clear that the men who would be taken to prison would be treated well and soon released.

Together, they chose Flight Sergeant Cyril Copley to continue on to freedom because he was on one of his last missions before leaving India. The three American agents were also selected to leave. Otherwise, they would face harsh punishment and possible death because they were there to assist in espionage against the Japanese. Smith and Gildee would also continue on to freedom.

The remaining aircrew would become prisoners of war. Smith and Gildee explained the situation to the others, and the men who were leaving left any useful belongings to the men who would be jailed.

The four prisoners were taken away a few hours later while the rest stayed in hiding until it was dark. The general in the Siamese Resistance, along with a group of well-armed fighters, escorted them to the local office of the American headquarters of the Office of Strategic Services (OSS). They stayed for four days at the local OSS, receiving medical assistance for their wounds and resting and enjoying the food.

On June 11, 1945, the men waiting at the OSS were joined by two others: Major Kellogg, an American pilot who had made his way to freedom after being shot down 13 months before; and Private Olle, an Australian soldier who had escaped from a Japanese work party on the Burma-Siam railroad. The Japanese commonly forced prisoners of war to work on war projects like the railroad.

Shortly after midnight on June 12, 1945, all of the men were given revolvers and guns for a bus trip to an airfield where they would be picked up. But as they started to travel, the bus repeatedly backfired as it went down the street, drawing attention. The driver quickly made his way to the police station where they had been before and another bus took them back to the OSS headquarters.

After they made another hasty change of bus, the group was again on their way to an airfield about 80 miles away. At dawn, three small aircraft landed at the airfield. Soon, the men were flying towards another airstrip in a more remote region two hours away, where the escapees were hurried into hiding in a bamboo basha tent.

In the morning, Smith checked the runway, which was about 3600 feet long, and sent his report to Allied headquarters. In the morning of June 14, 1945, a Dakota from No. 357 Squadron arrived. Flight Lieutenant L.G. Lewis piloted the Dakota to a good landing on the runway, but the soft ground at the end of the airstrip gave way. The Dakota's wheels sank into the mud. The men approached the aircraft with apprehension. If the landing gear had been damaged, they would have to wait for another aircraft, but when the airmen looked at the wheels, they realized that it was not too serious.

The men on the ground pushed the Dakota free and back onto the runway. About an hour passed before the escapees were safely aboard the aircraft and on their way. There was a sense of relief as the plane landed at Rangoon, where it refuelled and then took off again. Partway through the afternoon, they landed at Alipore, near Calcutta, which was the headquarters of SOE. The escapees were taken to debriefing and were soon recuperating. Three weeks had passed since the plane crashed in Siam. Those four crewmembers who were sent to a prison were released only two weeks after they had been imprisoned.

Flying Officer H.V. Smith of the RCAF was awarded the Distinguished Flying Cross for the efforts he made in crash-landing the Liberator while injured and for saving as many lives as he had. The citation pointed out that he had remained calm. About a year later, Smith was also awarded the Croix de Guerre because he had flown seven difficult supply missions over French Indo-China.

During their trek to freedom, the men remained vigilant and focused. Yet like so many of these stories of escape and evasion, it wasn't only these traits that helped them to escape. They owed much of it to the co-operation and guidance of the local people and the police as well as the official resistance. The assistance of these people was crucial to their escape.

CHAPTER THREE

Canadians and MI9

DURING THE FIRST DAYS OF WORLD WAR II, IT BECAME CLEAR that the conduct of war had changed. The German Blitzkrieg could take control of enemy territories by rapidly travelling around the enemy's defensive forces and capturing their command headquarters. Many Allied units had no idea that they were surrounded and defeated because communication with central command was cut off.

The development of mobile military forces that could quickly surround their enemies created conditions that had never been seen before, including the capture of greater numbers of soldiers. During World War I, captured soldiers were sometimes blamed for being taken prisoner. During World War II, however, capture by the enemy was generally accepted as an accident, not as a failure on the parts of the soldiers.

British military intelligence organizations knew that escape for Allied service personnel who had been captured or were undetected behind enemy lines would be more likely if there was a secret organization to assist them. By the end of 1940, efforts were underway to develop an underground line of agents and safe houses for the Allied servicemen who were making their way back home. There were lines that took servicemen to Switzerland, Sweden, Spain or the Mediterranean, and, later in the war, to the coast of Brittany. The organization was coordinated in London through Military Intelligence 9 (MI9) and in the lowlands of France by the local French Resistance.

The role of MI9 was not to control or operate escape lines. These lines had to be operated by the local Resistance because they knew the culture and geography of where they were operating, making them the driving force for effective escape lines. The most successful members of the Resistance were young women, mostly those in their teens. They would guide evaders and escapees through crowded public places and to travel on trains. Even with the escapees' inability to speak the language, poorly fitting clothes and unfamiliarity with their surroundings, these young women were able to efficiently and safely help them to escape.

MI9 provided the money, arms and supplies that the Resistance needed to continue their work. A number of agents were specifically trained and brought into Europe to assist with the Resistance. These agents included radio operators who communicated with London and played a critical role in arranging for evaders and escapees to be picked up at various places. With their radios, the MI9 agents also coordinated the movement of supplies to the Resistance.

Trained MI9 agents had to operate with discretion at all times. They had identities as workers and professionals who had reasons to travel. The MI9 agents had to carry out their work in coordinating the escape lines while they worked at their identities' jobs. They had to be anonymous in the communities and arouse no suspicions. The MI9 agents had to have steely nerves—they were under constant threat—and show no signs of stress. The agents also had to be courageous in contacting strangers who might be able to help.

The activities of MI9 included instructing all personnel who were at risk of being captured behind enemy lines in how to evade the enemy. Aircrew members were told to get away from their landing site as quickly as possible. If they could get away, there was a 50 percent chance of evading the enemy and returning home. MI9 often pointed out that many who ended up in a prisoner of war camp regretted not taking advantage of the time after their landing. Too many servicemen did not understand how fast they had to start running. Often those who were captured had not followed in detail the instruction they had been given.

As part of their MI9 instructions, aircrew were told to search for a church or a remote farmhouse once they made it away from the landing site. It was important to avoid towns or larger urban centres. Those evaders or escapees making their way out of enemy territory would find allies in the clergymen, railroad workers or teachers. They were warned to approach a teacher only as a last resort, however, because MI9 thought teachers were possibly supporters of the Nazis or opinionated about politics. A priest was the best individual to approach because MI9 had no reports of a priest betraying someone who was evading the enemy. If an airman was able to approach a porter on the railroad, his chances of being swept into the Resistance were very high.

Once an evader or escapee was taken into the underground line established by the French Resistance and MI9, he was expected to do exactly as he was told for the safety of everyone involved in the escape line. Escaping servicemen often remained secluded in safe houses for long periods of time while travel arrangements were made, civilian clothes were gathered and forged documentation was prepared.

Not all servicemen adapted well to these rules. Some of them would pay little attention when they were given instructions for their transportation and would casually pull out cigarettes that were American or British as they sat in a crowded train station. Some airmen horrified their hosts because they would not remain in the safe houses and would walk around the town and even go to the cinema. A few evaders would insist that their hosts take them on a tour of the community as if they were tourists.

Sometimes, the fact that some Canadians and Americans could not ride a bicycle was surprising and caused great difficulties for members of the French Resistance. Many civilians in the occupied countries used bicycles for transportation. Escapees were often expected to complete some part of their journey by bicycle. In one case, Angus MacLean— who would later be a federal cabinet minister and the premier of Prince Edward Island—had to bail out of his bomber while over the Netherlands. A priest took MacLean to Belgium, where he was to go with a young woman in the Resistance to a railway station that was 20 miles away. The two were to carry fishing tackle and appear to be a young couple on an outing. When MacLean pointed out that he could not ride a bicycle, the young woman agreed to take him to the train station while he rode on the handlebars. The scene of the teenaged woman riding with a tall and much heavier man on the handlebars brought looks of amusement to all whom they passed.

As the war went on, the work of the Resistance and the MI9 agents became more difficult. The rationing of all items from food to clothes and footwear made the preparations for each escapee or evader more difficult. The simplest needs were difficult to meet. There were great risks involved in buying food and supplies on the black market even when those in the Resistance had the currency provided by MI9. The black market was unsafe. Many of the people who participated in it would take whatever advantage they could, including betraying people working for the Resistance.

Many people participating in the black market were driven by profit, unconcerned about how they got it. They provided information about the activities of Resistance members for money. In the end, members of the Resistance often used their own rations to provide food and clothes for the escapees. Many of them had to do without to assist the Allies.

The operations were always at risk of being exposed to the Germans by collaborators who were English-speaking Germans. A few cases existed where the collaborators were Dutch or Scandinavian. A single arrest would quickly lead to more arrests and the executions of people in the Resistance. In some cases, when these arrests occurred, the entire escape line would collapse and those who survived had to establish entire new networks.

There was a general desire by the MI9 agents to minimize the involvement of the French Resistance in helping escapees move along the line. By setting up communication that kept each group of helpers isolated from the other, all of the participants were safer. If German agents infiltrated the line, they would never learn more than what was occurring in a specific area. Sophisticated systems of communication were established where individuals would pass along information using coded messages. For example, a bookstore owner would receive a telephone call in which he would be asked if three books by Victor Hugo could be re-bound.

The storekeeper would say, "Yes, this would be fine." Later in the day another call would come asking if the store owner had any Victor Hugo. The reply would be that the store had three volumes. The first message told the store owner that there were three evaders or escapees to move on. The second telephone call confirmed that there were three men to be moved. If no men were in the safe house to move, the reply was, "Sorry, I have no volumes today."

The personnel who had to move through the line were taken to a designated place, such as a park bench, by one guide. Once they were seated, the guide would leave. The escapees would wait about half an hour for another guide to arrive and take them to their next location. The system had to be well coordinated, but it worked well with neither guide knowing who the other was.

Early in the war, an effective and relatively safe escape route went from France through the Pyrenees to neutral Spain. But the lines for escapees to Spain were long and slow. MI9 wanted to develop a faster route to the northern French coast in Brittany and then across the English Channel. By shortening the evacuation lines, MI9 believed that those involved would face fewer risks. The French lowlands did not provide the protection that was needed to move large numbers of men out to sea. Also, the Germans heavily guarded the area because they expected that the lowlands would be the most likely landing place for an Allied invasion. It was decided that the escapees would have a much better chance along the rough coastline of Brittany. The geography would provide the escapees with coverage from the German patrols, which were increasing as the war years passed and a cross channel invasion became imminent.

When MI9 was developing its system of moving evaders and escapees from France, it used an earlier program called the "Helford Flotilla," which was established in the autumn of 1940 by the Special Operations Executive (SOE). The SOE effort effectively moved its agents and supplies to and from the Brittany coast. The effort to develop an escape route out of Brittany was becoming more intense later in 1942 because there were a large number of airmen staying in safe houses all over Brittany. At the same time, the Spanish escape line collapsed when a French traitor assisted the Gestapo by infiltrating its base in Marseille.

A new agent had to be sent to re-establish a new line that could evacuate the airmen, but there were very few agents available to MI9. The agent chosen was one they already knew and who went by the name "Val Williams." His name was Vladimir Bouryschkine, and he was born in Russia, but his family emigrated to France and then the United States before World War II. He became a well-known basketball player and a physical trainer.

In 1940, he arrived in France as a volunteer with the American Red Cross. Williams worked with Donald Caskie, who was a chaplain serving in the Royal Navy. The two men assisted soldiers who had evaded Dunkirk. These men were moved through a line to Spain. Later, Williams took the cover of being the coach of the Monaco basketball team and aided the Marseille group that was run by Albert-Marie Guerisse, a Belgium medical officer. Guerisse was known as "Pat O'Leary," which was the name of one of his friends. He said he was a Canadian in the Royal Navy. On September 13, 1942, the line moved its first evaders out on a ship named the *Tarana,* which was made to look like a tuna trawler. It was shortly after this success that the Marseille line collapsed. Pat O'Leary fell victim to an infiltrator and was arrested and sent to a prisoner of war camp in February 1943.

Val Williams was trained in beach evacuations and in the rapid boarding and unloading of Lysander aircraft. He was prepared to return to France to link all of those people left in Paris and Brittany who had been a part of the Marseille line and to evacuate those who had been in hiding. Once the line was established, it would provide a rapid system of moving evaders and escapees across the English Channel to England.

Williams had a reputation for acting naively. He was too willing to tell casual listeners what he was doing. Given that there was a shortage of agents at the time, his reputation was overlooked.

By the time Williams arrived in France in early 1943, he had to find old contacts and establish an entirely new line that would collect all those in hiding and move them across the Channel to England. The operation was given the code name of "Oaktree." It was very dangerous because the Paris group had already been infiltrated. The Oaktree operation would have to establish a new organization in Paris. The landing site for the pickup of the evacuees was a stretch of beach at the base of a rocky cliff on the Brittany coast near the small community of Plouha, which was near the small port of Paimpol. A strong group of French Resistance members at Plouha would assist in the operation. The evacuation would have to be carried out in an area where there were German patrols on top of the cliffs.

In the operation to move escapees and evaders across the English Channel, there had to be good communication between those on the ground and those at sea. The boats had to land at high speed under the cover of dark at a specific point on the coast to load the evacuees. Raymond LaBrosse, a French-Canadian member of the Royal Canadian Corps of Signals, volunteered to provide the radio communication needed.

LaBrosse, who was 22 years old, had joined the Canadian army in 1940, shortly after Canada declared war on Germany. LaBrosse was recruited by MI9, which, like the SOE, recognized the value of French Canadians as good agents. They had a European manner and spoke French. Added to these strengths was the need to have agents in the field that had excellent radio skills.

Raymond LaBrosse was asked in the summer of 1942 to speak with a British officer from the War Office. The interview was extensive and covered many aspects of LaBrosse's background and his attitudes. This meeting led to a second interview with MI9 in London in August, where they asked whether Raymond would like to volunteer for clandestine operations in France, to assist Allied airmen who were evading the Germans. LaBrosse replied that he would volunteer and that he was confident and anxious to help more actively in the war.

The secrecy needed for Raymond LaBrosse's role in MI9 began immediately. When asked by his fellow signalmen at his camp in Sussex, England, about the meetings, Raymond replied that he was now working at a secret radio station in Scotland. Later, when his fellow signalmen saw him in London wearing civilian clothes and living at the Regent Palace Hotel during his training for MI9, he replied with the same answer.

LaBrosse was in training when the Allies suffered their immense setback at Dieppe. Adding to that the news of the collapse of the Marseille line and the infiltration of the Paris organization, LaBrosse realized how dangerous his operation would be. He and his MI9 colleagues would have to establish an entirely new organization in France. He knew that any of the old contacts who appeared to have been untouched by the Gestapo might have been left alone just so they could be watched by the Gestapo. The Gestapo may have obtained significant information, including names and places that they decided to use to stop any further activities.

Val Williams and Raymond LaBrosse were rushed through a training program that included parachute jumping and evasion. The two men then proceeded to a Royal Air Force station at Tempsford, England, where they would be flown to a drop location at night. Both Williams and LaBrosse felt increasingly tense. They would have to fly over occupied France in a Halifax bomber and risk being shot down a total of nine times— the first eight passes before they actually jumped were necessary because the pilots had to be absolutely certain of the drop site.

Val Williams carried on as he always did. Waiting night after night for a successful jump into France bored him. He demanded to go out to the local pubs to relieve the tension. When he was taken to a local pub, he loudly complained that the Royal Air Force was inefficient. The ruckus quickly brought the local security officers. They threw Williams and the personnel with him out of the pub. They were not allowed to return.

Williams and LaBrosse made a successful parachute jump close to the Forest of Rambouillet, just outside Paris. The supplies they brought for the operation, including a radio and bicycles, were parachuted near their landing site. After landing, they rushed away from the site and approached a farmhouse where a farmer nervously agreed to allow them to stay for the night. Although it put him in grave peril, the farmer allowed the two agents to hide their supplies at the farm until they had an operative in place in Paris.

Williams and LaBrosse had planned to go out the next day with the bicycles. The bicycles were to make them appear to be long-time residents since they had the bright yellow French licences, but LaBrosse's bicycle was badly damaged in the jump. Williams used his to go to the local train station where he bought a ticket to Paris. LaBrosse stayed at the farm at Rambouillet to get his radio working and contact London. The radio was also damaged, and he was not able to get it operating. In London, MI9 had no idea if the two had successfully landed or if they were going ahead with the operation.

Williams was given contact information for a lawyer in Paris, Paul-François Campinchi, who was from Corsica. He had played an active role in sending escapees and evaders along the line to Marseille and to the Spanish border. After Williams had his meeting with Campinchi, he started the process of finding volunteers to establish a new network of safe houses in Paris.

The former American Red Cross volunteer travelled to Brittany to visit the Count and Countess de Mauduit at the Château de Bourblanc. He arrived on April 10, 1943. Both the Count and Countess were Americans who agreed to co-operate with the rescue effort and to house the evaders and escapees. At the time, they were hiding 39 airmen, who had to be evacuated as soon as possible. These airmen were among a group of about 100 who were in various places in the region. The large number of airmen in hiding was causing problems. There was a continuous need to feed them and a real fear of detection as the amount of time they stayed in the area lengthened. Williams explained that it would take until May to organize a large evacuation across the Channel.

Unable to repair his radio, LaBrosse had to use the communication system set up by the Free French intelligence agency. The process was very dangerous because there was no way to assure the security of the lines. Through these communication lines, an arrangement was made for a new radio to be brought in from Spain. Raymond LaBrosse travelled to the Bordeaux train station to pick up the radio that was placed in the luggage office at the station. The radio was large and not disguised—more portable radios were not available until later in the war. Being caught with a radio transmitter meant that LaBrosse would be interrogated by the Gestapo and tortured. He would face execution for being a spy.

Once LaBrosse had the radio, he took the train back to Brittany where he was able to contact London. A mass evacuation was arranged for the night of May 29, 1943. The Royal Navy was to use a fast motor gunboat to go to the agreed upon place and pick up the evacuees. For the operation to be successful, there had to be superior communication, but the second radio that LaBrosse was using was not working well. The Royal Navy had to have the ability to make last-minute changes and communicate them to those on shore. If the radios were not working or not working well, they would not go through with the effort. It was much too risky. The operation was cancelled.

There were other reasons for the cancellation of the evacuation. There were reports that one of the French Resistance volunteers named "Roger le Légionnaire" was the one who changed sides and brought the O'Leary line to a close. He assisted the Gestapo with information about the Marseille escape line and was present for the arrest of Pat O'Leary. Information collected by MI9 suggested that "Roger le Légionnaire" was actively working with the Germans and was based in Rennes. MI9 was worried that this man knew a line was being established in Brittany and was turning his attention to the new operation.

MI9 also received reports that Val Williams was continuing as he had before with open conversations about the operation. Many of those involved in the escape lines later said Williams knew nothing about security and did everything he could to let others know he needed volunteers, just short of publishing advertisements in the newspapers across France. The news reaching "Roger le Légionnaire" could have come from Williams' indiscretions.

There were 86 airmen in safe houses in the Brittany area that had to be evacuated, but MI9 ordered Williams not to approach any of the volunteers who had been in the O'Leary line that was shut down by the Gestapo. Williams ignored the direct order and started contacting the old volunteers he knew to start moving the airmen to the south and to safety through Spain. Williams headed south with one Polish and two American airmen. He was travelling by train on June 4, 1943, when the Germans arrested him and the airmen close to Pau. The effort to bring Allied airmen home was shut down just over a week later when the Count and Countess de Mauduit were picked up by the Gestapo. The Germans also detained the airmen who were hiding at their Brittany château.

Raymond LaBrosse was in hiding when the Gestapo picked up Williams. He knew that he had no choice but to leave. The Gestapo knew that LaBrosse was part of the operation. It had to be closed down when it was established that Williams had the codes for the operation when he was arrested. The codes and other information about Oaktree were now in the hands of the Germans.

The only choice for LaBrosse was to escape through the organization developed and run by the Free French. In August 1943, LaBrosse travelled with 29 Allied airmen south through an escape line that took them to Toulouse, Andorra and then Barcelona. The Oaktree operation was a failure, but LaBrosse told the authorities that the plan to move escaping airmen across the English Channel could work. He had kept details about what worked and how a new effort could operate smoothly. The greatest difficulty was created by Williams' inability to communicate discreetly and secretly. With the information provided by LaBrosse, another operation would be planned, but this time the agents would be men who understood the importance of secrecy and security measures.

Members of MI9 who had felt the sting of failure in the Oaktree operation were much more cautious the next time around. Two well-trained and tested Canadians would drop into occupied France to organize and operate one of MI9's most successful escape operations of the war. The operation to evacuate Allied servicemen across the English Channel became as effective as LaBrosse had said it could be.

CHAPTER FOUR

Escaping Dieppe

By THE SPRING OF 1942, PRESSURE WAS GROWING ON BRITAIN and its allies, such as Canada, Australia and New Zealand, to directly attack the occupying forces in France and open a second front. Another front would relieve Russian forces that had been suffering from continuous German advances in Russia. The Allied response was the planning and execution of a raid at Dieppe on the French coast. The Dieppe raid in August 1942 brought approximately 4963 Canadian soldiers to that coastal landing. From that number, 2210 soldiers made it back to England. There were 1946 captured as prisoners of war, including the wounded. In the raid 907 Canadian soldiers lost their lives. Other than the disastrous number of dead and wounded, there were many long-term consequences of this event. A number of the Canadians who were left behind and then escaped and returned to England became effective agents in Military Intelligence 9 (MI9). The escape lines, which were developed by agents from the Allied countries working with the French Resistance, improved the situation for evaders and escapees—all those airmen who found themselves in enemy territory had a 50 percent chance of evading the Germans and making it back to England.

Four members of the Canadian Fusiliers Mont-Royal who had been taken prisoner at Dieppe and escaped were trained by MI9. This group included Conrad LaFleur, who was from Iberville, a town in southern Québec. The other three, Guy Joly, Lucien Dumais and Robert Vanier, were from Montréal.

The troops taking part in the Dieppe raid on August 19, 1942, rushed onto the pebble beach backed up by air and naval forces. The aim of the raid was to test the German defensives, to gain a foothold in France and to capture German prisoners who could provide intelligence. Once these goals were achieved, the Allied forces would retreat and prepare for a full invasion of France.

The tanks that might have provided some protection from the direct firing of the German machine guns and mortars were immediately bogged down in the deep, loose pebbles on the beach. Hundreds of Canadians died shortly after they stepped onto the beach.

Sergeant-Major Lucien Dumais was among the Canadian soldiers who rushed the beach at Dieppe to face a hail of German bullets and mortars.

Dumais, like LaFleur, Joly and Vanier, was with the Canadian Fusiliers Mont-Royal. It was early in the morning on August 19, 1942. The relentless fire from the Germans quickly stopped the Allied advance. The battle lasted hours.

Dumais was a no-nonsense muscular Sergeant-Major who effectively directed his men. Dumais' men were able to hold their position and sustain fire on the enemy. He was able to concentrate the fire, forcing the Germans who posed a direct threat to stay undercover and unable to return fire. When the retreat was called, many of them successfully made it back to the landing crafts. During the retreat, Dumais was in a position to help those who were wounded.

Sergeant-Major Dumais knew the Germans had to have known that the Allies were coming and had time to reinforce their defences. He felt angry and disgusted by the carnage he was seeing around him. As the order came to retreat, Dumais tied his handkerchief to the bayonet of his rifle and propped the butt in the pebbles and sand and worked to help the wounded around him. The handkerchief was yellow, but it was clear to the attackers he wasn't fighting anymore. Despite seeing many retreat to the landing craft and leave, he worked feverishly trying to help the wounded men. He had a clear opportunity to retreat himself, but he stayed.

Soon Dumais was marching with the nearly 1000 soldiers captured by the Germans. The men who could march on their own helped those who were wounded and could not. Lucien Dumais knew he was going to be taken to a prisoner of war camp. He shook his head as he thought about how the war had just started and for him it was already over. Dumais decided he would not stay in a prisoner of war camp; if he didn't try to escape, he would always wonder whether he could have made it. There was a risk of being shot by the German guards, but he decided to take it. As they marched to where they were to be transported on trains to the camp, they passed through a village called St-Martin-L'Eglise. The villagers gave the soldiers water, which was the first drink many of them had had in about nine hours.

Those who did not need medical attention were forced to march the rest of the day and then into the night. The captured soldiers were then allowed to sleep for a few hours in a partially constructed factory. Soon, the German intelligence officers systematically questioned them. After the interrogation, the march continued until the men reached a railroad siding. The captured soldiers were ordered to climb into the waiting cattle cars to be transported to a prisoner of war camp in Germany.

As Dumais walked toward the train car, he noticed that the German guards were riding in every third car. Dumais thought that he wouldn't be able to get away with such a heavy guard presence riding the train. He immediately talked to other prisoners who also wanted to escape. They set to work pulling the planks from the floor of the train car. They looked through the hole in the floor and noticed that the axle was set too low and no one could slip under it. They quickly placed the planks back onto the floor and started to pull pieces of wood off the windows on the right side of the car. The soldiers looked out the opening and realized that anyone who wanted to escape had to climb out and stand on the ledge of the train car. Then, at the right moment, they could jump to freedom. They had no idea what their chances were on the run in occupied France. As they worked on their plan to escape, they saw one of the prisoners in the next car signalling to the German guards. Some of the captives in that train car hurriedly approached the man and began questioning him. He said he was from Glasgow and was with the No. 6 Commando Group, but he had no hint of a Scottish accent and his English was terrible. The men in the car knew that no member of the No. 6 Commandos took part in the raid at Dieppe. They quickly concluded that the man was a German spy who had taken a uniform from one of the dead on the beach and climbed into the car with the rest to watch for escapes. Their first idea was to knock the man out and drop him through the hole they had just recovered. They didn't carry out this plan because it would be discovered, and there would be reprisals. They decided to move in close to the man and keep him there. If he attempted to alert the Germans, they would kill him. Many volunteered to help.

The train began to slow. The men looked out and realized that the train was negotiating a sharp turn to the left. The conditions were perfect for someone to make the jump, but it had to be fast. The train car would soon pass the turn. In a moment, Dumais and two other soldiers were out the window and standing on the narrow ledge preparing to jump. They noticed that when they leapt, they would be unseen by the cars ahead of them and behind them. But, more rapidly than they thought was possible, the train sped up and the rail was straight again. At such a high speed, the three soldiers would be injured or killed if they jumped. They clung to the side of the train car and pulled themselves in as tightly as possible. In the darkness of the night, they saw the lights of a village train station. They were certain that with the platform crowded with German soldiers, there would be an alarm called, but nothing was heard as the train passed with the three escapees hanging on in full view. The train continued on far too fast for the three to jump. In disbelief, they saw the lights from another village station come into view. For the second time, the three escapees pulled themselves tightly to the outside of the train car as it passed through the second station. The platform at the station was again crowded with German soldiers who did not alert the guards in the train that there were escapees on the outside of the car.

The train slowed as it climbed up a steep hill. The men leapt from the train. They hit the ground and quickly rolled down a steep grade and then came to a stop at the bottom of the ditch. Lucien Dumais was not sure where the other escapees were as he leapt to his feet and ran down a gully. He ran in a zigzag pattern because he saw and heard bullets fly by him from the guards on the train. He continued to rush down a gully until he came upon a thicket of brush. He dove into the thicket and waited a few moments as he watched the train slip into the night. The shooting ended.

Dumais caught his breath, expecting to hear a search party come after him with vicious Alsatian dogs, but there was no sound as the quiet of the night surrounded him. He experienced a strange and sudden feeling of freedom mixed with apprehension. He was sharply aware that he was in occupied territory where the enemy was everywhere and that he was still wearing his uniform. However, the feeling of freedom was real and grew stronger as he became more aware of the darkness around him.

Lucien Dumais stood up and started to walk in the same direction he had run. He wondered what had happened to his friends and started to whistle the regimental bugle call from the Canadian

Fusiliers Mont-Royal, *Un Canadien Errant,* that his comrades would recognize. There were no replies in the night. Dumais thought that they must be far away on their own treks by now. He picked up the pace of his walk to a near jog as he moved along the gully.

As the excitement of his escape faded, Dumais began to feel an intense thirst. He had not had anything to drink since he was given some water at the village beyond Dieppe. He heard the hushed sound of a stream running in the woods, which he followed. He was soon able to drink what he needed. He wanted to be more refreshed, so he stripped his uniform off and washed it. Dumais bathed and then pulled his wet, cold uniform on again.

Dumais continued on in the darkness and was surprised to find an orchard. He feverishly ate apples and pears. Once he finished, he put more into his pockets. He felt much better as he looked at the half loaf of German bread he had been given to use as emergency rations. He thought about how he would make his way in the next few days to the English Channel, steal a rowboat and paddle back to England. Dumais continued to walk in the darkness and soon came to a small village. He noticed that there was a house that was some distance from the rest, with a small barn behind it. *The barn is the best place to hide,* thought Dumais. He made his way into the hayloft where he quickly fell asleep.

When Dumais woke up in the morning, he saw the cold greyness of the rising sun and thought about how well he would do on his own. He knew that he couldn't go on for very long before he would be picked up if he wore his uniform. There were real hazards with stealing civilian clothes as well. Before Dumais and his companions were sent on the raid at Dieppe, they had received instructions about escape, which were vague and uncertain. The soldiers were told that the rural inhabitants might be unsympathetic or even hostile to the German occupiers. Escapees who came back in the early years of the war reported the cooperation they received from civilians. After these escapees' experiences were relayed back to the military intelligence authorities in England, the policies changed. Getting the assistance of civilians in occupied countries then became a central aspect of all planning.

Dumais was also told that his French-Canadian accent would be difficult for people in France to understand—that those who heard a French Canadian speak would assume he was a migrant worker. Despite these warnings, Dumais decided that he would have no chance of making his escape from France without help from the local people. He ran across the road from the barn and knocked on the door of a small house. A young woman answered the door. She appeared to be shocked by the sight of Dumais. The woman invited him in and told him she had heard about the raid at Dieppe, indicating that she understood he was one of the Allied soldiers who had gotten away from the Germans. She asked Dumais to wait a moment so that she could go check if he had been followed. He was suspicious and decided that if she did not return within five minutes he would run. In a moment, she returned and told him that he hadn't been followed. She invited him to eat and gave him a meal with wine.

As the two talked, Dumais realized that he had been very lucky to knock on the young woman's door. Madame Collai had already assisted soldiers who had to flee from the Germans. She had helped many people even though there were signs posted around the village stating that anyone caught helping escapees would be shot. Added to this, Madame Collai had three children who were also endangered by her assistance. Doing so, however, was her way to help free herself and her children from the Nazi occupiers.

As soon as they had finished eating, she set to work preparing Dumais to successfully escape. She called in her gardener whose name was Robert. Dumais was told to take his boots off, which he did and handed them to Robert. With skill and speed that indicated Robert had completed the task he had just been given many times before, he pulled out the knob nails from the boots to make them appear to be civilian boots. The boots were then covered in mud, to make them look like a farm worker's boots. Dumais took off his uniform and was given a badly worn-out shirt, a pair of old, oversized pants and a beret.

"I am indebted to you for your help," said Dumais. "I don't have a lot of time, and I have to get going right away if I want to make it to the English Channel."

"I didn't realize you wanted to go to the Channel," said Madame Collai.

"Of course," said Dumais. "That would be the fastest way back."

"If you actually make it to the Channel, how will you get across the water?" asked Robert.

"I'm going to take a rowboat. I'll have to steal one, but—"

"No," said Madame Collai impatiently.

"I know there are some who would agree with stealing—"

"No," repeated Madame Collai. "Your plan is no good. The coast is the most heavily guarded region in all of France."

"The Germans can't be standing heel to heel. There are ways through."

Dumais was surprised by the angry looks on Madame Collai and Robert's faces.

"You may as well as turn your self over to the Germans right now if you intend to go to the Channel," said Madame Collai.

"Even if you have help from the local people on the coast, you wouldn't make it out to sea," said Robert. "Even if you made it out of the harbour with a rowboat, the waters are extremely rough. I doubt you would make it all the way back."

"More importantly, you will need identity papers and permits to even get close to the coast. The Germans will stop you. If your papers are not right, that will be the end of you," said Madame Collai.

"I don't see any other way," said Dumais.

"Everyone who makes it back goes south to Spain and then Gibraltar," said Madame Collai.

"That's a long way," said Dumais.

"It's the only way," said Robert.

"There are willing helpers all the way," said Madame Collai. "You have to travel to Poitiers, which is at the demarcation line between Vichy France and occupied France. You'll have to be careful crossing the line, but once you're in Vichy, you will be safer. You just keep going south through Spain and to the coast."

After a long discussion, Dumais had to admit that he knew little about occupied France and that he had to accept Madame Collai's advice. The plan was that Dumais would set out the next day. After a good night's sleep, Lucien Dumais was prepared to travel south. For the trip, Madame Collai gave him a package that included a map of France ripped from a textbook, a razor and a bar of soap.

She also generously gave Dumais almost all her money and ration coupons for bread.

Dumais felt nervous as he walked to the train station wearing poorly fitting clothes. He would have to quietly move around the local population undetected. At the train station, he was careful as he quietly asked for a ticket to Poitiers. He realized that not only was he speaking with a French-Canadian accent, but there were many Anglicized words in his usual conversation. He had to carefully think about every word when he spoke. He received his ticket from the man in the booth and left relieved. It appeared that nothing out of the ordinary was happening.

Dumais made his way across the platform with his ticket, feeling better as he stepped into the train car. He froze as he came face to face with a German soldier staring at him. Without any suspicion, the German soldier glanced sideways, and Dumais found his seat. He relaxed as the train moved along until it came to a stop at Le Mans. A group of German soldiers boarded the train and started to ask every passenger for his or her identification and travel papers. Dumais quickly slipped off the train.

The Canadian soldier was walking in the country in the summer heat. He travelled along a road, taking care to find cover in the ditch or in the brush each time an automobile passed. Exhausted and hot, he walked up to a farmhouse hoping for the best. He introduced himself and was welcomed into the house and given a large piece of bread and coffee. He listened as the farmer and his wife began to argue in whispers. She was sure that he was a German agent who was travelling the countryside looking for those who would help escapees. Dumais thought it was amusing, but he realized that he should leave right away. Before he could excuse himself, the farmer asked him to leave. To keep things friendly, the wife gave him a bacon sandwich with a few boiled eggs.

Dumais made his way to the train station and bought a ticket to Tours, which was on the way to Poitiers. He climbed on the train, nervously watching for Germans. There were none. He made his way to his seat and continued watching as the train pulled out.

Soon, the train was at Tours. Dumais noticed a woman who needed help with her luggage. He helped her and started a conversation. They had to wait at the train station one hour for the train to Poitiers. He found out that she was on her way to Poitiers as well. She told him she lived near the demarcation line to Vichy France. She had come to the conclusion that Dumais was escaping from a German forced labour camp. Dumais went along with her assumption. He arrived in Poitiers late at night. He noticed that the entire train station was empty and decided to sleep on one of the wood benches.

With the first light of the day, he was up and walking south to Vichy France. Soon Dumais entered a small village, stopped at a farmhouse and asked the woman at the door for a glass of water. Dumais was asked to wait as she got her husband, who was working in the blacksmith shop. The heavyset blacksmith arrived shortly. Dumais told him that he was a soldier who escaped after the Dieppe raid. The man was very pleased to meet one of the soldiers who had taken part in the raid. He wanted to know all about the raid and how he had been able to travel over 250 miles when the raid had occurred just five days before. Dumais told the couple that his success had been entirely made possible by the helpful people he met along the way. The blacksmith offered to take Dumais across the line to Vichy. Dumais refused his offer because it would be too dangerous.

The man quickly drew Dumais a map of the line and how to cross. He put in detailed information such as where the guard posts were and where a gunner's nest was hidden high in a tree. Just as Dumais was about to continue his journey, a man arrived to pick up some farming equipment that the blacksmith had repaired. The man agreed to give Dumais a ride on his wagon to a place within a couple of miles from the line. Lucien Dumais spent the rest of the day waiting for nightfall, so he could make his move across the border.

In the dark, Dumais made his way across the line. He felt victorious as he walked southward certain that he had made it. He was surprised when he stepped into the path of a soldier who told him to stand still. Dumais quickly took 10 steps backwards. He turned and ran for a ditch and sprinted up it as fast as he could. Bullets flew by his head as he disappeared into the darkness. He didn't stop running until he thought he had gained about a mile on the soldier. He had no idea whether the soldier was French or German, but he didn't care. He continued to run until he found a hay-field where he covered himself as well as he could and slept.

In the morning, he was making his way along a road when a couple approached in a car. They stopped and offered him a ride. After he looked at them carefully, Dumais decided they were safe to go with. He accepted the ride to Lussac-les-Châteaux and was taken in by the local French Resistance. The French Resistance gave Dumais a set of identity papers and sent him along the escape line to Marseilles. Once Dumais was in Marseilles, he made contact with the American consul who secretly passed him along to those operating the O'Leary escape line. When the arrangements were made, he was then sent to Perpignan with a number of other escapees. The group took a short ride on the train to Canet-Plage, which was near the Spanish border.

Moving as a group, they made their way to the southern coast of Spain. On October 5, the group assembled at a designated beach where rowboats arrived to take them out to the *Tarana*, the Royal

Navy ship that was painted to look like a Portuguese tuna trawler. They were making their way to Gibraltar when German naval patrol boats challenged them. The crew played their roles as Portuguese fishermen and were quickly on their way again. Once Dumais was in Gibraltar, he was flown back to London. He arrived about two weeks after the first group of Canadians, which included Conrad LaFleur, Guy Joly and Robert Vanier.

Amidst the slaughter of Dieppe, Robert Vanier found himself in hand-to-hand combat during which a German soldier thrust a bayonet into his back. Conrad LaFleur received shrapnel wounds to his legs. Guy Joly was assumed to have been wounded and was transported with other Allied soldiers to a military hospital operated by the Germans in Rouen.

After receiving treatment, the wounded were moved onto a train that would take them to a prisoner of war camp in Germany. The three men had agreed that they were not going to accept that the war was over for them and decided they would take the first chance to escape. They decided that they would stay together and help each other because attempting to escape alone was impractical for men who needed ongoing medical care.

Even though the train they were placed on was heavily guarded, the three Canadians had an advantage because the German guards were not as vigilant watching the wounded as they were for those who were able bodied. The men felt an intense need to make their way to freedom. They believed they had much more to contribute to the war effort. As the train left Rouen, the three watched for the best opportunity to jump. The train had not picked up speed when it had to slow down again for a bend in the tracks. Vanier, LaFleur and Joly had no idea where they were, but they decided to jump into the darkness.

The three men knew their best chance of escape was to stay in the countryside where local farming families were more likely to help. Many who wanted to fight against the occupying forces often ignored the Germans' threats of execution for helping escapees. Helping Allied soldiers was accepted by many in occupied France as necessary to gain their own freedom. To many French citizens, not helping those evading the Germans meant accepting the occupation.

Because they were weak and exhausted, the three made little progress in the darkness. In the early morning they made their way to a field where the local farmers were harvesting hay. They approached in their blood-stained uniforms, struggling to walk. The farmers were cautious because of the heavy penalties for assisting Allied servicemen escaping. They were also glad to help those who had participated in the Dieppe raid, which many

French citizens saw as a sign that they were not alone in their struggle against the Axis powers.

The French farmer and his wife worked quickly to give the three men civilian clothes to replace the ragged blood-stained uniforms they were wearing. The farmer knew that Dr. Beaumont, a local physician, was a contact for escaping Allied servicemen. The men would have to be moved south toward Paris, and then on to the demarcation line to Vichy France and then to Toulouse.

Once the three arrived in Paris, they had nearly no contact with the French Resistance and found a hotel in the slums. The hotel clerk did not ask any questions of customers who stayed only one night. Robert Vanier was weak from his wound and the loss of blood. His companions knew that they would have to treat the wound on his back with disinfectant before a serious infection set in. They left Vanier on the bed in the room to go out and find disinfectant. When Vanier asked how serious his injury was, LaFleur and Joly told him it was a simple flesh wound. Vanier didn't believe them and persisted in asking how serious it really was. He got up from the bed and went to the mirror where he saw that the wound ran much of the length of his back. He fainted. He remained there until LaFleur returned and helped him back to the bed. LaFleur applied disinfectant and dressed the wound with bandages he had made himself.

The journey of the three escaping servicemen was a strange mix of being helped and venturing on their own. In one case, they sat beside three German soldiers on the Metro in Paris as their French Resistance guide escorted them to the Gare d'Austerlitz, the train station where they would board the train that took them south.

Three days after leaving Paris, the men appeared to be fugitives under arrest when they crossed over the demarcation line to Vichy France. They were, in fact, being driven across by police officers who were Free French agents. Once the three were in Toulouse, they hid there for three weeks. Robert Vanier was taken care of by a woman who was a doctor with the Resistance. His injury had become badly infected.

Once Vanier had recovered enough to walk, the group travelled to Marseille, which was, at the time, the main gathering centre for escaping Allied servicemen. They were a part of the O'Leary escape line that moved men to the south coast through Spain and to Gibraltar. The success of the escape line meant that there were a large number of hidden escapees in the city. Over 250 French Resistance volunteers worked to support the needs of those in hiding. In Marseille, the three Canadians were feeling well. With their ability to speak French and blend with the local population, they were allowed to travel in the French countryside to assist in gathering supplies.

Escapees were then moved to Pau and Perpignan, where they were picked up by the ship *Tarana* that took them to safety in Gibraltar. From there, they were taken to England. The *Tarana* was painted to resemble a brightly coloured Portuguese tuna trawler after its first trip to Gibraltar because the military grey colour was causing too many questions in Spain. German patrol boats were also a constant threat. The crew of the ship dressed in clothes that made them look like Portuguese fishermen.

Early in September 1942, the three Canadians arrived at Perpignan for their turn to be transported to Gibraltar on the *Tarana*, which had already successfully picked up a large number of Allied airmen and servicemen. While the three waited to be picked up, they stayed in a safe house that was owned by a Jewish family.

The three Canadians waited on the beach at Canet near Perpignan with more than 40 Allied escapees on the evening of September 13, 1942. The *Tarana* arrived right on schedule, and they were soon in Gibraltar. LaFleur, Joly and Vanier then boarded the *Malaya*, a battleship that took them to Greenock in Scotland on October 6, 1942.

When Conrad LaFleur, Guy Joly, Robert Vanier and Lucien Dumais arrived in England, military intelligence officers questioned them as they had all other escapees. The four told stories of working their way to freedom independently. All of them were comfortable and capable of appearing to be French citizens. They were clearly resourceful and quick thinking. All were asked to train with MI9 and return to occupied France. The four agreed and began their training.

CHAPTER FIVE

Canadians Return to Occupied France

MANY OF THE MEN WHO SUCCESSFULLY ESCAPED DURING World War II did not return to their regiments or squadrons. Many agreed that they had faced enough risks from their ordeals. Another practical reason to not send a returned aircrew member back over Europe was that they knew too much about the escape lines and the French Resistance. If they were captured, there was a risk that they may reveal important information to the enemy.

Other Canadian escapees, such as Conrad LaFleur, who was from Iberville, and Guy Joly, Lucien Dumais and Robert Vanier, who were from Montréal, were asked to enter training to return to occupied France as Military Intelligence 9 (MI9) agents. All four took part in the failed Dieppe raid: LaFleur, Joly and Vanier had escaped after being captured by the Germans; Dumais had made his way back to England after escaping and evading capture.

Agents from MI9—the military intelligence agency that coordinated the escape of servicemen and agents from occupied countries—interviewed the four soldiers in London following their successful escapes. They were given a period of leave to recover before they returned to their regiment, the Canadian Fusiliers Mont-Royal. Once they were back with their regiment, Canadian intelligence agents interviewed them again. These escapees told stories that identified them as the kind of men who were needed to head escape efforts. They were quick thinking and adaptable to any situation. They had the capacity to handle the stresses and dangers of the work as agents for MI9. They were French Canadians who could speak the fluent French needed to operate in occupied France.

The Canadian intelligence agent asked if the men were willing to transfer to MI9 and become active agents in occupied France. They would assist in creating and maintaining escape lines that would help personnel like themselves evade the Germans and return to England. The men interviewed knew that it was accepted practice that they would not be allowed to return to active service with their regiments. Usually, escapees would be given desk jobs for the remainder of the war— they would not be allowed to participate in action that would risk capture as a combatant. Only exceptional opportunities would change this fate for men like LaFleur, Joly, Vanier and Dumais. They were also attracted by the idea of helping the war effort immediately while others in their regiment faced exercises and training until the invasion of France finally came. LaFleur, Joly and Vanier were also privates and faced few other options if they stayed in England in the regular services. These three agreed and entered the service of MI9. They wanted to help those who had assisted them in evading the Germans. Their return to occupied France would be one way they could do that. Dumais did not join MI9 until after a period of training in North Africa.

When LaFleur, Joly and Vanier agreed to become agents for MI9, they began training. They were in a small group that included servicemen who were Dutch, French and Italian. The training was sped up because the need for new agents was great. The group of trainees faced the expectation that they would quickly become proficient at wireless operation, evasion, disguise and the use of small arms. It was also necessary for them all to be trained in parachuting—many agents were dropped behind enemy lines at night. As the training proceeded, Joly became ill and had to leave the program. He was unable to return to occupied France.

With their training completed, Conrad LaFleur and Robert Vanier were given their briefing before they were sent into France. Each of them were sent to different parts of France to contact and work with the French Resistance in order to move out French Resistance and British agents, who were at risk of detection by the Germans. They had to be evacuated as quickly as possible as the capture of active agents was the greatest risk to operations. Agents with information who were captured and turned over to the Gestapo faced torture and, potentially, revealing critical information.

Once LaFleur and Vanier were in place they would assist other agents to complete various assignments. Using the same lines, they would also take all airmen who found themselves behind enemy lines and help them escape to freedom.

Vanier's partner was Yves le Henaff, a Free French Resistance agent who had volunteered for service with MI9. The two played an important role in radio communication for a sub-circuit operation led by the French Resistance. Vanier would be the radio operator. The two men would be working for George Broussine, who was responsible for getting Raymond LaBrosse, a Canadian MI9 agent, out of France as the Gestapo closed in and shut down the operation LaBrosse was working on.

Yves le Henaff's father owned a large fish cannery, located at Quimper in the province of Brittany. The cannery would le Henaff's and Vanier's base for the operation. In May 1943, le Henaff and Vanier parachuted into an area that was hidden by woods. The two went to the nearby village that le Henaff was familiar with. He simply telephoned his brother who was surprised to hear from him. His brother had been a French army officer. He agreed to have them stay with him as they prepared for their operation.

Once they were settled in, the two travelled together to find good landing areas for Lysanders to deliver supplies and to take escapees back to England. The Lysander was an effective aircraft that had its wing set above the cockpit. The aircraft could land and take off in a short distance.

The men travelled south, across the demarcation line to Vichy France, to find the best landing sites. As Vanier travelled on his first assignment, he noticed the questioning glances that came when his papers were inspected. He looked at the papers he had been given in London and compared them to what others had and realized that they were dangerously lacking in detail. He hurried to get the advice of those in the Resistance who would know what to look for in identification and travel papers. They agreed with Vanier's observation and quickly worked to have better false papers made for him.

The men making the identification papers for Vanier knew he would have to travel a great deal. They agreed that he had to have a legitimate trade that would also keep the Germans from asking too many questions. Vanier was given the identity of a specialized veterinary assistant who was called a "de-wormer." There were very few men who were trained in the area of de-worming cattle, and the demand for such a person was great. He would have to travel everywhere in France to perform his work. At the same time few occupying German soldiers would want to have an extensive conversation with him. The assessment that the Germans wouldn't want to observe his work or inspect his luggage too carefully was found to be true.

With such identity papers Vanier was able to make many trips from Paris across the demarcation line to Vichy France escorting British, South African and American airmen. On two occasions Vanier was stopped and detained by the German authorities who wanted to examine his papers. Each time he was carrying the big, bulky suitcase that contained his radio, which would have been a clear giveaway that he was an agent. But after the Germans examined his identity papers and looked at Vanier, they were all too eager to have him collect his suitcase, unopened, and leave.

On another occasion the Germans saw Vanier on a bicycle and arrested him. He didn't wait too long before he bolted, leaving the bicycle behind with the Germans. He made it to safety because of his fast action. The Germans looked the bicycle over carefully, but they found nothing to identify it and could not trace it to anyone.

With all the arrangements in place, le Henaff and Vanier were able to organize several pickups of MI9 agents, Special Operations Executive (SOE) agents and other Allied agents, such as MI6 agents. They decided to use Lysanders for the pickups, although doing so was risky and only a very few agents could be moved each time. There was always a risk of the Lysanders being shot down, and when landing, the planes could be spotted by Germans who would move in quickly to apprehend everyone.

With so few people transported by Lysanders, it became clear that another escape route was needed. Broussine—the leader of the French Resistance who was coordinating the escapes—had organized several English Channel escapes on the coast in southern Brittany. Planning turned to the establishment of a more secure way to get larger numbers of escapees across the Channel.

The planning was urgent because Pierre Brossolette, who was a prominent journalist, broadcaster and member of the Socialist Party before the war, was on the run from the Gestapo. The Germans were closing in on Brossolette, who was also an important member of the French Resistance. Emile Bollaert, a prominent Gaullist, was working with Brossolette and also needed to escape. Gaullists followed the political philosophy of Charles de Gaulle who opposed the Vichy regime. Brossolette and Bollaert wanted to report to General de Gaulle the efforts that had been made in the French Resistance to assist the Allied forces for when the invasion of France began. The two were in hiding, waiting to be picked up by a Lysander. Unfortunately, however, France was in the middle of harsh winter weather that had grounded the aircraft used for the escapes. A coded message was broadcast each night on the British Broadcasting Corporation to let le Henaff and Vanier know that no aircraft would be sent that day.

It appeared that there would not be any support from England, making the situation more intense for le Henaff and Vanier. The two decided to carry out their own plan. They decided that their best chance was to get a boat and make the crossing themselves. The men knew that the Germans were watching the boats that were available very closely. Le Henaff decided to use the money that had been parachuted to him to purchase a boat. He found the owner of a small fishing vessel, named *Jouet des Flots*, who was willing to sell it. It had been out of the water for about two years, and the seams had opened up. So the owner slipped it into the water to allow the wood to expand with seawater. Many of the seams did close as they became wet, but the boat was not ready to set out to sea when the owner accepted the money for it. The owner didn't mention that the boat was in such poor shape to le Henaff and Vanier.

The two men hurried as they planned their winter escape across the English Channel. The two men faced difficulties as they searched for the best place to launch their escape plan from. They needed a remote place on the Brittany coast that was beyond the intense patrols of the Germans. They turned to the Cap Finisterre, which was isolated, but the remoteness came at a cost. It was in the area known to be one of the stormiest coastal regions of the Channel. Added to this difficulty, they would be setting out in February 1944, the time of year that presented the most difficult weather conditions.

The arrangements included 26 Allied airmen who had to be evacuated as well as six French citizens, which included Pierre Brossolette and Emile Bollaert. This group was assembled from Paris and transferred to Brittany. The voyage, set for the night of February 3, 1944, was to include le Henaff and Vanier. Conditions on the Channel could not have been worse as they set out. The boat cleared the rocks in the darkness, but the seams of the boat opened up as the crew worked the vessel into the heavy waves. The pump couldn't keep up with the water rushing into the hull. The strain from the overloaded boat and the heavy seas caused the motor to stop running. They were drifting back to the shore as the light from dawn started to rise over the eastern horizon. The crew had to carefully direct the craft back with paddles, hoping that the German patrols did not spot them. The boat was obviously out of commission from the storm as it laid anchor near the shore. Few on the coast gave it a second look. The crew struggled to bring the sailing mast down and lay it out over the rocks toward the shore. Those people onboard the boat walked along the mast to shore.

After the airmen, Frenchmen and Vanier and le Henaff made it to shore, they agreed to go in different directions to reduce the chances of being caught by the Germans. Many of them made their way to a small coastal village called Plogoff. Many of the airmen did not have identity papers, which made the situation even more dangerous. Added to this, Vanier had lost his papers and radio in the wrecked boat.

The results of this failed attempt to cross the English Channel were disastrous. Shortly after the group agreed to travel in different directions, a few were quickly apprehended by German patrols for not having the necessary papers to be in the highly restricted coastal area. Once the attention of the Germans was drawn to the area, they put together what had been attempted the night before. Nearly all of those involved in the escape attempt were soon arrested.

Late on February 4, 1944, Pierre Brossolette and Emile Bollaert were arrested by the Germans, initially for not having the needed permits issued to those who worked in the coastal area. Soon, their true identities were revealed, and they were charged with other crimes. The arrests included le Henaff who was taken for interrogation. The French Resistance found out that le Henaff was in a prison in Brittany, and an effort, led by Vanier, was started to break him out. The Resistance had already attained co-operation from the guards at the prison and were preparing to move on the prison when le Henaff was suddenly taken to Paris. Finally, the decision was made to move le Henaff to a prisoner of war camp. The Germans had detained so many people to be moved to prisoner of war camps that there was a shortage of railroad cars. The German authorities pushed ahead with their plan, and they loaded prisoners in cattle cars by piling them on top of one and another. Many, like le Henaff, died of suffocation long before the train made it to the camps.

Robert Vanier struggled to make it to shore from the doomed fishing boat, *Jouet des Flots*. He had lost his radio, identification papers and shoes. His clothes were wet, but he continued on his way up the coast for three days without food. He was on his way to contact a Resistance worker whom he had met in the area. Once he had made contact he heard that an unknown agent, who was being called a "captain," was arranging another escape route across the English Channel. The "captain" was Georges le Cornec, who was the Plouha Resistance leader. He heard about the work of Vanier and agreed to meet him at a hotel in Guingamp, which is a town in the Côtes-d'Armor in Brittany.

The Canadian MI9 agent Lucien Dumais, who had known Vanier when they were with the Fusiliers Mont-Royal, travelled with le Cornec to the meeting at Guingamp. He didn't know Vanier was the agent they were about to meet. As le Cornec and Dumais approached the hotel, they were prepared, with their pistols in hand, for Gestapo traps. The three met in the corridor of the hotel. Dumais and Vanier were surprised to see each other. Neither knew the other worked for MI9. The two embraced and exchanged greetings. It turned out that an operation was underway and on the next night they would have a group leave from a beach close to Plouha. The three men agreed that Vanier should be among those taken back to England. The next night Vanier joined other men who were picked up from the beach and brought back to England on a Royal Navy gunboat. The operation was a success.

Conrad LaFleur was among the group of Canadian escapees from the Dieppe raid who made it back to London and was trained by MI9. During his training by MI9 it was clear that Conrad was quick thinking and highly capable, but unsophisticated. When the time came for LaFleur to be briefed for his assignment in occupied France, he was told that he would participate in an operation named "Marathon." In this operation many would have to be rescued during the invasion of France. No one knew the exact date of the invasion, but plans were underway for D-Day beginning in the summer of 1943. The operation that LaFleur was to participate in would provide a hiding place for Allied soldiers and aircrew who would not be able to escape south to Spain or Switzerland because the roads, bridges and railroad would have been bombed and destroyed.

Operation Marathon would see the establishment of safe places for Allied servicemen to go to hide in the countryside. It was always safer to hide Allied servicemen in the countryside because there was often a cooperative population, and a better supply of food existed for large numbers of men. The cities were dangerous because they were under constant patrols by the Germans. There was always a chance that collaborators would expose those staying in safe houses. The hiding places would be near railway stations in regions where there was an effective organization of French Resistance groups. The refuges for the servicemen would also have to be away from areas that would have a significant accumulation of German forces. As the numbers of Allied servicemen grew, they would travel to safe camps that would be established for Operation Marathon.

LaFleur was also instructed that while he was working to establish the hiding places and camps for Operation Marathon, he would also work with local French Resistance groups and MI9. The goal here was to maintain the escape line that had been established and to work with others to set up more escape lines. LaFleur's area of work was in the northeast of France. At the time there was a build-up of escapees in hiding in the area who needed more opportunities to make their way south.

There had been an escape line operated in this area called the "Comet" line, which was operated by the Belgium de Jogh family. The new line that LaFleur was going to support with his skills, including radio operation, was run by Belgian army and air force personnel who had been trained in England and had come back to the area.

LaFleur and his partner Count Georges d'Oultremont jumped into the area they would be working on the night of October 21, 1943. They made their low-level jump from a Sterling bomber near the village of Fismes. Count d'Oultremont had been working on the "Comet" line before he arrived in England to work with MI9. D'Oultremont was a guide for the "Comet" line when the Gestapo discovered its operation, and he had to flee to Spain himself.

The first thing that the two had to do was locate nearby fields that were flat enough for Lysanders to land. There was a need to get the Lysanders into the area to move agents who were being tracked by the Gestapo. They also had the assignment to find well-hidden areas that were surrounded by forest that could be used to establish camps where Allied servicemen could stay during the invasion. These camps would be in the Fretteval and Ardennes areas. They wanted to move those Allied servicemen that were in hiding in the lowlands.

Once LaFleur and d'Oultremont had located a safe landing field for the Lysander, the first Lysander arrived to drop off two Belgian officers who were to establish the escape line. LaFleur followed up with a message to London to report that the operation to deliver the two had been successful and that contact had been made with French Resistance agents in Paris. Two women were recruited in Paris by d'Oultremont to act as guides for escapees travelling south.

In another operation LaFleur identified a field in Aisne close to Coucy-le-Château for a pickup of aircrew by plane. The operation was a success with two Lysanders arriving and picking up three United States Army Air Force crew and two from the Royal Air Force (RAF). These kinds of operations were risky and were usually used only for agents of Special Operations Executive (SOE) and MI6. Usually the airmen were moved south to Spain or Brittany.

The main work of LaFleur and d'Oultremont was to improve the escape line alternative to the "Comet" line and establish possible sites for escapee camps. LaFleur made regular radio transmissions until suddenly they were interrupted. The Gestapo rushed into his hiding place at Reims because one of the husbands of the guides they recruited collaborated with the Germans. He told them where they could find LaFleur. LaFleur was at his radio the moment that the Gestapo broke the door in, but without hesitation, he grabbed his pistol and shot two. At the moment of the shooting he was able to run to the door that led to the basement that led to another door at the back of the house. He paused a moment to throw a grenade into the corridor behind him, where another German Gestapo officer was closing in on him. He ran as fast as he could and arrived at a hotel where a friendly worker moved fast to provide the escapee with a black suit, a hat that matched and a pair of glasses. The employees from the hotel gave LaFleur a ride to the train station where he was able to get a ticket and board a train, walking right by a German police officer who was standing on the platform. The train to Amiens was crowded, but LaFleur walked boldly into a car where a number of Germans were seated and made himself comfortable.

LaFleur made it to Amiens, where there was chaos because a RAF bombing raid was underway. He left the station and made his way to contact Dr. Beaumont who had treated him and Vanier after the Dieppe raid when they were escaping France. Dr. Beaumont immediately sent him to a doctor who was near Amiens so that he could be hidden. The members of the "Comet" line made the arrangements, and LaFleur was guided to Paris. From there he was taken through the line to San Sebastian, which is on the Spanish frontier. He made it into Spain and then to the British consul located in Barcelona, where a MI9 agent took charge of him. Soon, a flight was arranged, and LaFleur was taken to London where he was awarded a Distinguished Conduct Medal.

Canadian Raymond LaBrosse had already been an MI9 agent in France when he was partnered with Val Williams. At that time they attempted to establish an escape route from the Brittany coast to England. The plan, named Oaktree, failed, and LaBrosse returned to England through Spain. He never stopped advising MI9 that a cross Channel escape plan was viable. LaBrosse was among the very few that requested to return to occupied France to make another attempt to establish the cross Channel escape route.

MI9 agents often had additional skills that were critical for the success of the operation that was being set up. Raymond LaBrosse was a French-Canadian member of the Royal Canadian Corps of Signals, and he was well trained in the operation of radios. Radio skills were critical for communicating with London in the coordination of boats that arrived for escapees waiting on the beaches along the Mediterranean or later, the English Channel.

MI9 agreed to send Ray LaBrosse back to France with another Canadian agent, Lucien Dumais, who was one of those who had escaped after the Dieppe raid. He was not among those who quickly agreed to return to France as an agent for MI9. Dumais was proud of the effort at Dieppe made by his regiment, the Fusiliers Mont-Royal. In fact, he took exception to the negative account of the raid by the newspapers in London. He responded by sending his own positive account to the newspaper using a different name. The censors were able to quickly find out that Dumais was the writer of the letter, which was considered a breach of security. Although Dumais wanted to return to his regiment, he was assigned to North Africa for further training in response to his attempt to have London newspapers print his version of the Dieppe raid.

Dumais found himself in service with the British First Army. He was assigned work that included horseback reconnaissance into areas that were well behind enemy lines. He was exceptional at these duties but was sent back to England after four months. Dumais began to have second thoughts about where he was as the uneventful daily routine of regular service in England left him feeling listless. He decided to pursue the offer from MI9 and contacted the Canadian Military Headquarters in London in mid-1943.

MI9 agreed to have Dumais begin working as an agent and decided that they would arrange a dinner meeting between him and Ray LaBrosse who had arrived back in England a short time before from the failed Oaktree operation. They were placed in the same living quarters, so that they could size each other up. As they exchanged stories about their past, their reluctance to work with a partner faded. Both wanted to work alone, but each knew they needed a good reliable partner to be successful. As time past they realized that they were closely matched and that together they had a good chance of success.

When they decided that they could work together, MI9 placed them in training for their operation. The two men had complementary traits that made their partnership one of the strongest teams of agents in occupied France. Dumais was quick talking and could made fast and exacting decisions in difficult situations. LaBrosse was reflective and brought the careful planning and caution that would be needed for this operation to be successful.

LaBrosse was already qualified in parachuting, but Dumais was not. Dumais was sent to Ringway to take parachute training. Both men were given additional training in radio operation in the new compact radios that had been developed for MI6 and given to MI9. Their training included cryptology, which was needed for the increasing sophistication of operations in occupied countries, and communications. There were additional lessons in the quick use of pistols in confined areas, forcing locks, hand-to-hand fighting and techniques in quickly escaping from a pursuer.

It was important for the agents to be completely comfortable with the new identities they were given, so that there would be no hesitation at all when they were addressed. Hesitation when one was spoken to was a sure way to identify an agent in disguise. Lucien Dumais' false papers gave him the identity of Lucien Desbiens, who was a mortician who lived in Amien. Raymond LaBrosse, as the radio operator, would be carrying a radio at times. To cover for the radio if challenged by police, he was given the identity of Marcel Desjardins who was acting as a sales representative for a company that was selling electrical medical equipment. Like all other agents, both men were given several other false identification papers, so that they could rapidly change their disguise if they were betrayed. To simplify memorization, the names and the dates of birth remained the same.

The two had a clear mission to establish an effective cross Channel escape route to England for those escapees who had to be evacuated from occupied France. During the final days of preparations, the two were instructed by the Royal Navy about what was possible with their Royal Navy gunboats.

MI9 had attained a high level of sophistication in preparing their agents for operations. Dumais and LaBrosse had a microfilm that contained the code needed for communication; they had disguises that made them appear indistinguishable from the local population. Their coat pockets were cluttered with old tickets from the Paris Metro. The two had old, tattered road maps and fountain pens, which were really effective tear gas weapons.

LaBrosse and Dumais were ready to be transported into occupied France and attempts to land them began. The conditions had to be just right for the landings because bad weather and flooded fields would substantially increase the chance of capture upon arrival. MI9 preferred to fly them and their equipment in with a landing rather than parachuting everything to the ground below. In the past, equipment was often destroyed from parachuting. The two men had to climb aboard aircraft and prepare to land at night four times before the pilots came down on a meadow that was near Chauny, which was about five miles north of Paris. As they watched the aircraft take off from the meadow, they knew they were on their own to make Operation "Shelburne" a success.

Once they arrived, LaBrosse and Dumais were sheltered by a manager of a nearby sugar factory. The operation plan was that they would stay in hiding until the local resistance volunteers could make sure that the German authorities in the area were not aware of the landing. After a few days they were given the all-clear sign and their host took them to the local train station where they boarded the train to Paris. They had the name of a new volunteer—a young woman who had already assisted a number of Allied airmen along the escape route. The men had no trouble locating her as she worked as a hairdresser at a shop on Rue des Capucines. The woman's assistant heard about her work and agreed to keep LaBrosse and Dumais at her house.

The two women discussed the plan to establish an escape route to Brittany with LaBrosse and Dumais. They agreed to be a part of it and to provide escapees and evaders who passed through Paris with safe houses and other items that were needed. The two were given very little information because both LaBrosse and Dumais operated on a strict rule of having their volunteers know only what they needed. This secrecy would provide security to everyone in the escape line because if anyone of them was arrested and tortured by the Gestapo they would be able to tell them just about nothing.

The women agreed to gather as many Allied escapees as possible and house them in Paris until they were given specific information about where they should be sent for pickup. Dumais and LaBrosse were particularly careful about security. Both insisted that the women carry out the instructions that they gave them exactly. Among the instructions, which the men repeated, was that they were not to tell anyone anything, except to those who were also known resistance volunteers. For their own safety, the two women were to tell other volunteers absolutely nothing more than what was essential to carry out their tasks. The two women agreed to this, but Dumais and LaBrosse were not satisfied that they truly understood. Both men told them the absolute minimum of information.

The need for their restraint and secrecy was quickly proven. Both women were arrested the very next day. They were completing the transfer of several airmen to move along the escape line to Spain when they were apprehended at the Gare St. Lazare train station. With the loss of these two women to the cause, Dumais and LaBrosse had to start establishing their escape line again.

The effort to find new volunteers brought LaBrosse to Paul-François Campinchi, who held the position of clerk for the Perfecture of Paris. LaBrosse knew Campinchi from his earlier efforts in occupied France when he was working with Val Williams. It was a very risky contact for LaBrosse to make because it was not known if Campinchi had played a role in the arrest of Williams or if he had been identified during the interrogation of Williams. There was also a possibility that he had remained completely unknown to the Gestapo. Dumais and LaBrosse had to quickly establish a line of volunteers who could start bringing escapees to Brittany. MI9 did not give them any other names to contact in Paris. With no other choice, LaBrosse approached Campinchi and was immediately taken in by him. Campinchi provided hiding places for the two and began organizing the Paris activities for the Shelburne operation. The luck of Dumais and LaBrosse had taken a turn for the better. As time passed, it was clear that Campinchi was extremely capable and vital to the successes of the operation.

The success they had made had to be relayed by radio to London. LaBrosse set up his radio in Paris, but he was not able to make contact, so he had to find another place to establish contact. He packed up his radio and took it in its suitcase to Normandy on a train that was loaded with large numbers of German soldiers. When he arrived, he rented a small hotel room and set his radio up again. This time he was successful in making contact, and short messages were sent and received by LaBrosse.

Campinchi used his position and contacts in Paris to establish an entirely new set of volunteers who could fill every needed role in the escape line. The Paris operation needed an organizer who would work to find and run a series of safe houses. Another very capable worker would be needed to pull together all the supplies that were needed, such as civilian clothes and food. In the conditions of occupied France, attaining regular items like old clothes and food was very difficult. Another volunteer was needed that could carry out printing and forging the identity and travel papers needed to travel in occupied France. A group of doctors was needed to treat the wounded and ill escapees. Others were recruited that could teach the escapees how to act, so that they would appear to be migrant workers.

The three men, Dumais, LaBrosse and Campinchi agreed to institute the highest level of security by splitting up and making contact only when they had to. They followed a very stringent process of giving all their volunteers only what information they needed to carry out their work. These measures were absolutely insisted upon by LaBrosse who had experienced the failure of his earlier operation with Val Williams because there had been no attention paid to security by Williams.

To make the escape line operate well, they also needed to establish a number of mobile groups that would travel to northern France to contact, pick up and bring escapees to Paris. Paris volunteers were in charge of this part of the operation.

With the Paris network quickly coming into operation, the difficult task of setting up the receiving establishment in Brittany had to be completed. The work to establish the Brittany network was risky because of the efforts of the Germans to militarize the coast. Special papers were needed to travel anywhere on the French coast. Added to this problem was that the Germans had forced many French people who lived in the coastal area of Brittany to move away. The operation demanded that the escapees had to move into the area and be housed until arrangements could be made for their safe evacuation on a Royal Navy gunboat. The evacuation would have to be carried out on moonless nights when the German patrols would not see what was happening.

The plan for the Shelburne operation was to use the contacts made by LaBrosse during the earlier Oaktree operation in the village of Plouha. That operation had the same objective of evacuating escapees from the Brittany coast. LaBrosse was lucky as he found some of the people who had agreed to work on the earlier operation. A medical student who he met during his earlier operation in Paris had graduated and was now a doctor in the village. Le Cornec was a French soldier who had agreed to volunteer for the earlier operation and was still in the area. They were given a safe house to stay in while they set up their operation in Plouha. They travelled to the agreed pickup site, which was a secluded beach about five miles north of the village. This beach had been chosen by the Royal Navy for the operation, and it was clear to Dumais and LaBrosse that it would work well. They had to carefully make their way past a few German patrol houses that were nearby, but doing so appeared possible. The beach itself was made up of shingle and sand, which made it ideal for the landings of small boats. The 65-foot-high cliffs were effective for cover from the German soldiers who patrolled the beach, but they also presented an obstacle to the escapees who would have to make their way down them. All the details of the beach were described to London by radio.

The plan called for a coordinated effort that would see significant numbers of escapees arriving at Saint-Brieuc, which was a town close to Plouha by train. The main organizer in Saint-Brieuc was the local controller who had duties to make sure that wartime ration regulations were followed in the local population. He also organized the safe houses for the escapees in the area. Le Cornec had organized groups of volunteers for various tasks that ranged from assisting the evacuations on the beaches to housing the airmen. It was le Cornec's men who supervised the dangerous trip from Saint-Brieuc to Plouha by train. All of the escapees were taken by the volunteers who worked with le Cornec to safe houses and barns to hide until the night they would be taken to the beach.

With everything in place for the first operation, LaBrosse radioed London and asked for a date for the first evacuation. He also asked for a more powerful radio, money, weapons and more supplies to be delivered at the same time.

The escapees were called "parcels," and when Dumais and LaBrosse arrived back in Paris they found that Campinchi had already collected 16 parcels to be evacuated. There were 12 airmen from the U.S. army air force and four from the RAF. These men were instructed to act as migrant workers on their train trip to Saint-Brieuc. They all appeared to be exhausted and slept as the train made its way. Once they were in Saint-Brieuc and taken to safe houses, the next step was to transport them to Plouha. Le Cornec's men took these men in groups of two or three on the night train. As the first evacuation was coming to completion, two British Intelligence agents were added to those who would be picked up on the beach. Ironically, the man who worked at night to take the parcels to their safe houses was François Kerambrun. He was a mechanic who spent his days driving the Germans around the coastal region in the same truck that he used for the escapees. He was very bold because he knew that the Germans treated everyone who helped the Allied forces the same, regardless of how many they helped. He took 19 escapees on one trip. When he was told this action posed far too great a risk to him, he pointed out that the penalty for helping one escapee was the same as helping 19.

For a successful evacuation, conditions had to be right—a moonless night, the tides at the right level and good weather. These conditions were not in place when the first pickup was planned for December 15, 1943. The pickup had to be postponed until conditions improved, but the gales that began about that time continued for 10 more days. The Royal Navy were finally able to make a landing on the beach on the night of January 29, 1944. The men who were waiting in the area were nervous as time passed.

Dumais and LaBrosse realized that the operation in Brittany was in capable hands, so they returned to Paris and continued their work avoiding meetings with each other as much as possible. There was an agreed signal to let those who were in the Shelburne operation know that everything was set for a pickup. The British Broadcasting Corporation French Service would announce "Bonjour tout le monde à la maison d'Alphonse." Later this message was repeated at 2:30 AM, which told the operators that the Royal Navy gunboat had just left from Dartmouth.

This message launched the final part of the plan that saw guides pick up the escapees from all the

locations in the area and start them on their way
to the beach. Once they arrived at the area above
the beach they were met by Dumais who told them
that they would form a line. Each man would walk
behind the other holding the coat of the man in
front of him. They would all move down to the
beach together. As they made their way down
the cliff, they would remain completely silent. All
of those in the assembly were keenly aware that
there were German patrols in the area, and many
fought to suppress their nervous excitement.

On the beach Dumais gave the agreed flashlight
signal out to sea and received a signal back. Once
the two rubber boats approached the shore there
was the exchange of coded words that identified
each. Next was the rapid unloading of money,
weapons and supplies. After 15 minutes the operation was completed, with the supplies unloaded
and the escapees slipping into the darkness on
their way to Royal Navy Motor Gun Boat 503.
Soon they were safely back in England.

Dumais and the French volunteers collected the
supplies and made the short trek to a nearby farmhouse. They waited in the darkness until 6:00 AM
when the German curfew ended and quickly
returned to their own houses.

The first successful evacuation brought a change
in status for MI9 and its leader Airey Neave. The
many failures of the service to that point had left
it under a cloud of suspicion. With such a bold

success, many congratulated Neave and saw MI9 as an effective military intelligence organization.

Dumais and LaBrosse returned to Paris to prepare for the second evacuation. They continued to face risks and dangers. As it became increasingly clear that there would be an invasion in France, there were increased German patrols on the coast and the efforts to find active agents in occupied France increased. In one situation, Dumais was carrying a suitcase full of money when the police stopped him and asked him to provide his identification papers. He kept his composure as his false identification papers were carefully scrutinized. The officer found nothing wrong with the papers that had been presented and waved him on without checking the suitcase he was carrying. In the same way, LaBrosse was leaving a cinema and saw a collection of trucks outside when he exited. He was herded into the trucks like the others for a random interrogation at a German police office. He remained calm as the police checked his papers and asked him questions. The police found nothing out of order and released him.

One of the main dangers that faced LaBrosse was his need to carry his radio transmitter to a location where he could make contact with London. Until he received a better radio—and later several radios that could be left in various places—he faced a grave danger of being discovered. The Germans were also using equipment that could locate the direction of radio signals, and if any transmission was too long, they could close in quickly. He had the cooperation of the stationmaster at Gare La Chapell who allowed him to set up his radio in his office. The risks were substantially reduced when LaBrosse had radios in Paris and in Brittany, so that he could travel without carrying a transmitter.

The greatest danger that faced Dumais and LaBrosse happened when they were suddenly confronted by Val Williams, who had escaped from the Rennes prison and was helping a Russian officer escape. LaBrosse was nervous—it had been Williams' lack of understanding of basic security that had doomed the earlier Oaktree operation they had worked on together. There was a constant risk that Williams would act against the rules of security and bring about the collapse of the Shelburne operation. With few options, Dumais and LaBrosse were forced to enter Williams and the Russian officer into the Shelburne escape line. Williams was still a big security risk—he continued to announce his presence with actions like openly smoking English cigarettes when on the train from Paris to Saint-Brieuc. Adding to the danger was that there was an intense and coordinated effort on the part of the Gestapo to find Williams.

The second evacuation from the Shelburne operation occurred on February 28, 1944. This operation brought in more supplies and took out 19 escapees and two agents, one of which was Williams. On this trip the first RCAF airman could have been a part of the evacuation, but the French police stopped and then arrested the airman and a RAF pilot at the Saint-Brieuc train station. On the same operation Kerambrun was driving his truck, which was loaded nearly to capacity when he came to a German roadblock that was partly built. Kerambrun started to pull it down, but he was stopped by two gendarmes. Kerambrun was prepared to kill them if they wouldn't let him past, so he told them exactly what he was doing and the two agreeably let him pass.

With such successes the Shelburne operation was receiving larger numbers of escapees to transport back to England. The numbers of airmen who were coming down and needed to be transported back was increasing rapidly as the invasion in Normandy was getting closer. There were even more bombing runs than before. At the same time, perfect conditions were required on the Channel for an operation to go ahead because it would have to be a black night without a moon, the tides had to be right and the weather had to be good. There continued to be increased risks when too many escapees were in hiding because they were increasingly edgy and difficult to keep hidden. They also needed to be fed and have clothes provided.

Dumais and LaBrosse decided that the best course of action was to move these men along the traditional escape lines to Spain. To do so, they had a new recruit, who was a civil servant in Paris, contact the Basque underground in northern Spain to act as guides through the Pyrenees. There was no difficulty in making the arrangements because they were offered a very generous fee for the service. The 30 men successfully made the trip to freedom. The Basques were very willing to participate again, but Dumais and LaBrosse had moved the large number of men out and now concentrated on the Brittany operation again.

The pace of the efforts intensified as the numbers of airmen who were in hiding grew. By 1944, the bombing operations had increased, and Liberators were shot down regularly. Each one of these aircraft had 10 crewmembers. The higher demand for a much larger number of escape operations was seen when there were nearly 75 airmen hidden in Paris who had to be moved quickly. The resources of the resistance volunteers were being taxed, and because the escapees were human, they were unpredictable. The dangers increased daily.

Dumais decided that the efforts of the Shelburne operation had to be increased substantially. He radioed a proposal that called on the Royal Navy to carry out three rapid operations that would move about 25 airmen on each one. These operations were to take place on March 18, 24 and 30. The machinery of the Shelburne operation kicked in to move the men to the coast. By the end, 115 men had successfully found their way onto a Royal Navy gunboat bound for England.

In London, Neave had the opportunity to advise the Americans that many of their airmen, who had to bail out of their bombers on various raids, were being returned within a month, while in some cases they were returning only days after they were shot down.

The result was that more escapees were being sent through the Shelburne operation, and it was growing in size, requiring more volunteers and resources. The operation's success was, in a way, a dangerous development: the larger the organization, the more people involved, and the more resources needed meant that there was a much greater chance of discovery. Dumais assessed the situation and had a message radioed to London that there had to be a slowing down of the flow of airmen through the operation—he needed time to increase security measures. His opinion that there shouldn't be any more pickups for a few weeks was accepted.

Dumais took the time to search the coast on bicycle to see if there were any other secluded beaches that they could launch a fishing boat loaded with escapees from. He found that much of the coast was very heavily guarded. No possible place existed for them to set up such an operation.

In June 1944 Dumais and LaBrosse had a new problem. The Germans planted land mines along the top of the cliff over the beach they used for the operation. The two men carefully considered what to do. A solution was found when Joseph Mainguy, a French merchant marine captain, volunteered to find the mines and place a stick by each one with a white cloth attached. It was agreed that they could not remove the mines because the German patrols would realize what was going on. With this completed, a successful operation was later carried out on June 16.

On June 6, 1944, the Allied invasion of Normandy began. Dumais and LaBrosse were ordered the next day to travel to Brittany because the continuous bombing was rapidly destroying the train tracks. Soon, civilians would be barred from travel. It was also clear that Dumais and LaBrosse would be much more useful if situated in Brittany during the period of the invasion.

To get to their destination the two bought bicycles on the black market in Paris. They soon were on their way to Saint-Brieuc, which was about 250 miles away. On the way to the coast, a German artillery sergeant decided he wanted Dumais' bicycle and stopped him. He waved LaBrosse on and took Dumais' bicycle. Dumais went on foot to the next German military police post and made a complaint that the artillery sergeant had stolen his bicycle. The discussion turned into a yelling match. Finally, the German police agreed to give Dumais a ride the rest of the way to Saint-Brieuc. He arrived hours before his exhausted partner LaBrosse.

As the invasion pressed beyond Normandy and on into the lowlands, the German forces in Brittany were being reduced because many of them were transferred to German units fighting the Allies elsewhere. The German troops who remained were becoming increasing suspicious of those around them.

Most members of the French Resistance now knew about the Shelburne operation. With fewer Germans to track them and to stop the activities, those working in the operation were acting openly. Because the Gestapo didn't have the ability to call in large numbers of troops on operations, members of the Resistance were prepared to use arms against Gestapo members. The operation was quickly becoming a ferry service for those who had to come and go.

On June 16, 1944, both Dumais and LaBrosse carried out a very successful operation, when six military intelligence agents were brought to France and were taken into occupied France for their assignments. On this operation, no escapees went back to England. Dumais and LaBrosse could have chosen to return to England, but they decided to stay in occupied France. Both found each farewell to another group of escapees increasingly emotional because they were exhausted and unsure what to expect. After the escapees cast off, they would have to carefully step through the minefield and make their way back to Paris, where they would live with the threat presented by the Germans who were everywhere.

In July 1944—only a few days before the last movement of escapees through the Shelburne operation—the operation was seriously threatened with discovery by the Germans. The members of a patrol, made up of White Russians and Germans, were drunk and decided to burn down a farmhouse that had been a hiding place for airmen waiting for their chance to go to the beach. There was no one in the house at the time. Because of this fire, Dumais made sure that the Resistance volunteers he was working with were well armed as arrangements were made for the final cross Channel evacuation. They were all prepared to resort to open fighting if the last operation was interfered with.

One of the final evacuations was made up of 18 escapees, with most of them being fighter pilots who had been shot down on their raids during the invasion. Many of them were attacking German ground transport when they were shot down. Two more evacuations were carried out at the end of July as agents and other escapees were sent back to England.

Once the escape line out of Brittany was no longer needed, Dumais and LaBrosse turned their attention to assisting the local Resistance in fighting the Germans who were still on patrol. As the final evacuation was underway, LaBrosse was at his command post to radio London if anything went wrong. As he waited for the operation to be carried out, he heard two Halifax bombers fly over very low. He ran from his post and used his flashlight to give the OK signal in Morse code. The bombers made a circle and came back when LaBrosse sent the OK message again. In moments, 30 parcels were dropped from the bombers. The parcels made up a full shipment of arms and ammunition for a band of Maquis—Resistance fighters—which was some distance away. LaBrosse mistakenly supplied another local Maquis with the arms. Soon, the Maquis who were supposed to receive the arms arrived to demand their weapons and ammunition back. LaBrosse calmed them down by immediately radioing London to ask for another shipment of arms. Soon, both bands of Maquis had the arms they needed to fight the Germans.

Dumais and LaBrosse fought with the local Resistance against the Germans as the United States Army arrived in Brittany. A squadron of American tanks arrived at Plouha. The night before the Germans had pinned down the local Resistance fighters at Plelo, and the fighting had continued in the area. LaBrosse told the Americans about the situation, and they headed to Plelo, where they attacked the Germans with Dumais and LaBrosse fighting alongside them.

With the fighting in Brittany over, Dumais assisted the Americans, who could not speak

French, as they worked to establish law and order. There were many claims of collaboration against locals and many violent vendettas that people wanted to settle. Dumais worked with the authorities to rapidly sort out the differences and establish order.

Once order was established, Dumais found another assignment in rescuing more escapees. He became a part of a special operation to rescue more than 150 servicemen. They had been hidden in the Forest of Freteval by escape line organizers such as d'Oultremont, LaFleur and Campinchi as well as others. The operation used modified, cut-down vehicles and buses. The escape was daring—the group of servicemen was brought through the enemy's lines.

The partnership between Ray LaBrosse and Lucien Dumais was perfect as each provided what was needed for an effective and successful escape line operation. The extraordinary success of the cross Channel escape route was clearly a tribute to their abilities and courageous efforts.

CHAPTER SIX

Shot Down and Escaped

DURING WORLD WAR II, MANY PILOTS AND AIRCREW WERE shot down behind enemy lines and in a remarkable fashion, quickly evaded the Germans before they could be captured. Escape lines—developed by Resistance groups in the occupied countries of Europe—assisted people escaping from the Germans. As well, Military Intelligence 9 (MI9) established escape lines in co-operation with the locals. The local people who were discovered helping the escaping aircrew were often executed. For many people living in occupied countries, the desire to help the soldiers working to bring freedom to them was strong. All of the Allied personnel who did escape and made it back to England agreed that their success was largely because of the help they received from the people along the way.

There were also stories of those who made it to freedom without entering any of the established escape lines. Here too, those pilots or other aircrew understood that it was necessary to find local people who would help them as they trekked to freedom. The local people had to provide the Allied soldiers with civilian clothing, food and a means to travel to the next destination. Many escapees who made the successful trip were quick to react to their situations, were able to find co-operative people and agreed that luck was on their side.

One airman who made it to safety without contacting or using established escape lines was Flight Lieutenant Julian Sale. He was born in Ontario and received his education in Toronto before joining the Royal Canadian Air Force (RCAF). Sale was the captain of a Halifax bomber of No. 35 Squadron that was given the mission of a bombing run to Duisburg during the night of May 12th to the morning of May 13th, 1943. He was stationed at Gravely, which was close to Cambridge, England. Sale's crew was ready, and they took off before 10:00 PM.

The Halifax took off, and the crew was on their way without incident. The flight took the bomber across the Zuyder See (Zuider Zee) and beyond. At the point they were about to turn to head south where the target was, a German fighter appeared and began an attack. The bomber was torn up rapidly by the fire of the night-fighter, leaving it badly damaged. Sale could see that there was no way that the bomber could turn and make it back to England. He quickly gave the crew the order to bail out, which they did. Sale then made his own way to the hatch, but he didn't make it as the bomber exploded throwing Sale into the clear. Sale's parachute opened, and he drifted downward in the darkness. He came down on a pine tree and was dangling from his parachute. As he worked to grab the tree and release himself from the parachute, Sale realized that he had lost one of his flight boots. He knew that there was no way he could retrieve the parachute from the tree and decided to leave it where it was. If he was going to be successful in escaping the German patrols that would be looking for him, he had to get down the tree and find a safe hiding place. Once on the ground, he unclipped his life jacket and threw it down. He pulled his one flight boot off and took his sock off to put it on the foot that didn't have a boot.

He quickly set out to the west because when his bomber blew up, he knew it was very close to the Dutch and German border. If he was in Holland, he could approach a farmer and have a good chance of being hidden and sent on his way to freedom. If he was unfortunate enough to have fallen on the other side of the line and was in Germany, he would be in hostile territory where the local farmers would hand him over to the authorities. He came to a forested area that looked out onto two farms that were close together. He rested in the brush and decided to watch the area when the sun came up. He listened carefully to find out if these people were Germans or Dutch.

The day was warm and quiet, with little activity at the farms that would suggest which side of the border Sale was on. He remained where he was hiding as he was not going to take any unnecessary chances. He took care to determine which way west was. He waited and remained vigilant until it was dusk. In the dark, Sale was on his way again. He travelled 20 miles along trails and rough roads. It was dawn, and he noticed a thick-forested area ahead, which he slipped into to hide for the daylight hours.

Sale had found a churn the night before and had taken enough milk to fill his water bottle. He ate a few Horlicks tablets that he had in his pack for such times. Sale rested and thought about how far he had travelled. He looked at the landscape and decided that he must be in Holland. As dusk began to fall, he approached a nearby farmer for food and better footwear. The Dutch farmer was nervous because he knew both who Sale was and what the penalties were for helping him. He took Sale into his house and gave him some food and found a pair of clogs that fit him. The farmer was so nervous he insisted that Sale leave right away because the Germans had harsh punishments, including torture and execution, for those found helping Allied airmen. He showed Sale the way to Arnhem, which was south toward France.

Walking along in the clogs, Sale approached several villages. When he passed through them, he took off the clogs because they were making noise as he walked. Each time he took them off he noticed more blisters. Once the sun began rising again, he found a wooded area to hide for the day. He felt great relief as he dropped the clogs off his feet because his feet were blistered and painful. Sale would have to stay where he was as he had walked 40 miles in the previous three nights and needed to rest.

It was May 16 when he came to the edge of a small village. He decided to approach a house and knocked at the door. He was able to let the family know that he was an Allied pilot and needed help. They were fearful, like the first farmer he met. They brought him in and gave him a set of clothes, including new socks and shoes. They were not able to speak English, so the son went out and brought another boy who could speak to Sale. He was told that the people were fearful in the area because the Germans had previously discovered that the locals had been helping Allied airmen. They had arrested some of the people in the village. The family wanted Sale to surrender to the Germans, thinking it was the best thing to do. Sale didn't agree with this idea. They accepted his decision and agreed to have him stay that day and the next, letting him have a bed in the attic. He was well fed, and when it was time to leave in the evening, they gave him a large map.

Feeling confident with his new clothes and shoes, Sale walked during the day on better roads. As he walked he ran right into a German officer who was stranded because his car had broken down. With a confident look, Sale walked up and assisted him by pushing the car to a better location. The grateful officer saw no need to ask Sale for identification papers.

Sale knew there was a greater risk of being caught in larger centres. He decided to make his way around Arnhem and travel north to Oosterbeek because he had to find a bridge that crossed the Neder Riji. As he walked along, he saw the railroad bridge that linked the train from Arnhem to Nijmegan. Sale carefully looked around—it was dusk and he thought the bridge was unguarded and started to cross it. A soldier called out for him to stop, but he jumped off the bridge onto the bank and ran as a bullet whipped by him. He ran as fast as he could and was safe, as the soldier didn't follow him.

Sale made his way up the bank in the darkness, checking each boat that he discovered for one that was not chained in place. He didn't find even the smallest craft to use. Instead, he stripped all his clothes off and packed them tightly in his overcoat. He placed his coat on a few planks of wood and waded into the river, pushing it ahead of him. Once he was on the other side of the river, he dried off and pulled his clothes on. Then he was on his way, making it to the River Waal near Druten. As the early morning dawned, Sale came across a ferry that was crossing the river. As he approached, he met a Dutch boy who told him in broken English that the ferry was operating freely and that he could pass on it with the right money. Sale gave the boy a British half-crown for the pennies he needed. Sale paid his fare and was taken across the river.

As Sale looked at his map, he knew more obstacles lay ahead. The next was the River Maas. He arrived at the river's banks later that day to see another railroad bridge. He approached, much more carefully than at the first railroad bridge he had attempted to cross. He met a number of Dutch workers who were friendly and understood his situation. They told him it was a private bridge that was used for local industry. They gladly agreed to guide him across it.

Once over the bridge, Julian Sale saw a village, just beyond the river. He knew that he had to get more help, so he approached a house that was standing alone and away from all others. A schoolteacher, who was able to speak in broken English, opened the door. Sale was given a bed for the night, food and new socks. The next day after Sale got on his way again, he had barely started when he was stopped in the street by a Dutch police officer who demanded to see his identification papers. Flight Lieutenant Sale saw no other way of getting out of the situation, so he simply explained that he was an Allied airman who was on his way back to England. In uncertain French the police officer told Sale that he must be a Frenchman who was on his way from Germany back to France. Sale agreed—he had a rudimentary ability to speak French—that this was the case and they shook hands. The officer smiled, saying good-bye and good luck.

Feeling exhausted and hungry, Sale noticed a house near a church as he approached St. Oedenrode and knocked on the door fully expecting the local priest to answer. To Sale's surprise, three elderly women stood before him. He was immediately asked to come in for a meal. He explained to them who he was, and they listened with great enjoyment to the story. They were happy to help one of the men who was risking his life to free them all. They had him stay for two days to rest and prepare for the next leg of his journey. They were able to find a better pair of boots for him. They also were able to provide a better road map and a bicycle. Before he left they gave him a three-day supply of food. The women carefully told Sale where he would have to go to cross the Belgian border undetected by the Germans.

On May 22 at 3:00 PM, Julian Sale was nearing the border on his bicycle. Instead of moving across it quickly, he took the time to approach a Dutch family and asked them if the Germans were patrolling the area. They said that the Germans were not on the border at the time, and it was safe for him to pass. Sale felt better as he passed the checkpoint where there could have been Germans, but there were none. Soon he was stopped by two Belgian police officers who said they had to check his papers. Sale told them who he was and that he didn't have any papers. They were friendly and told him that he had a problem with his bicycle because it had a blue Dutch registration plaque on it. He would have to either get rid of the bicycle or get a Belgian plaque. The plaque he needed was described by the police officers. Sale didn't want to lose his bicycle, so he used a cigarette package to make a plaque that appeared to be Belgian. It would work as long as no one looked too closely at it.

Sale had decided that he would travel south as aggressively as he could because he believed his basic French and the goodwill of the people would get him to Spain. Staying on course, he was able to bicycle through Louvain and Charleroi. He had travelled about 100 miles by the end of that day and was very close to the border. He pulled his bicycle into cover and hid for the night.

The next morning, like so many times before, Julian Sale approached a farmer and asked for help. The farmer was very happy to walk with Sale through Grandneu, a village that was on the border with France. By doing this, Sale was able to pass into France without attempting to go through a guarded post. He also avoided crossing the frontier areas that were guarded by the Germans.

As he peddled southward into France, Sale realized that he had been on the road for 11 days and had managed to travel about 200 miles. He continued to hope that he would cross the path of an escape line volunteer who could help him, but so far he was still on his own. He looked at the map he had been given and planned to peddle along the back roads in rural France east of Paris. Each night he would have to risk contacting a farmer in hopes of being given a place to sleep. Sale never had a problem being accepted by the farmers who would provide a meal and place in the barn to sleep. Each day, as he prepared to head out onto the road on his bicycle, the farmers would give him the food he would need for the day. As he passed through Laon to Sens and on to the line that marked the frontier to Vichy France, Julian Sale had several punctured tires that forced him to push his bicycle to the next small town where they were fixed. At one point he had to have a pedal fixed as well.

At every opportunity Sale asked what the local licences for bicycles looked like, so that he could use paper, tin or other material to make it appear that he was a local. Sale realized that the earlier luck he had with local police would not necessarily continue in France. He was constantly watching for the local police, especially in the towns he passed through.

Sale was aware that heavy patrols were on the demarcation line that separated Vichy France from occupied France. As he bicycled just south of Bourges, Sale saw a local farmer. Sale stopped and identified himself and asked if the farmer could help him cross the demarcation line. The farmer was very happy to help and knew that there was an unguarded bridge nearby. He guided Sale to it and wished him well as he passed into unoccupied France. Sale felt intense desire to push as hard as he could to get to Spain and decided to try and travel 100 miles each day. He achieved his goal and arrived in Castre on June 1.

Extremely exhausted, the flight lieutenant arrived at Revel the next day and found a sympathetic farmer who was happy to have him stay as long as he wanted. Sale stayed in the relative safety of the farm for three weeks to recover from his trek that had brought him over 500 miles in the previous eight days.

At the farm Sale met a Frenchman who had just attempted to escape across the frontier to Switzerland, but he had found it to be very heavily guarded. He had no choice but to turn back and arrived at Revel to consider how he would escape. Both men agreed to make their move to the south and into Spain together. They faced a trip south to the border and through the Pyrenees.

They both knew that there were not the same patrols in Vichy France that there had been in occupied France and decided that the best chance of success was by train. They set out on June 21 for Toulouse. They boarded a train there that took them to Carcassonne, where they had to transfer to another train that travelled on to Quillan. They had to take a bus for the last leg of their trip to Belcaire, which was in the Pyrenees foothills.

The two rented a room at a hotel and then looked for a guide that could take them over the mountains to Spain. A guide was found who was arranging a group that included another six men who also wanted to go to Spain. The guide wasn't experienced, and by the end of June 24, the day they set out, he was lost. The group had to camp out in the mountainous climate before attempting to continue their journey the next day. On the next day they faced a steady climb, and by midafternoon they were about two miles from the border with Andorra. The weather was becoming cold—they had to cross a mountain range at about 7000 feet. The guide and others turned back while Sale and his partner decided to push through the snowdrifts to go over the top and down into freedom. The two succeeded making their trek over the top of the mountains by the late hours of June 25 and continued on until they came to a small hut occupied by a shepherd. They stayed in the hut and continued on their way the next day to make it to Canillo, a small town in Andorra. But the two still had to travel into Spain, and they heard in the town that the border was well guarded.

The local people in Canillo knew that the men needed help to get into Spain. The local men told them that an active smuggler in the area would be able to get them into Spain and through the countryside to Barcelona. The smuggler and his helpers agreed to take them and that night they were given a car ride very close to the Spanish border. The group got out of the car and in the darkness walked through the mountainous terrain into Spain. The overall trek lasted 10 days and brought the group through 90 miles of mountainous wilderness until they arrived in Manrea. The mountainous hike was the hardest part of Sale's trip. He was completely exhausted by the time they found a place to stay in Manrea. The guide knew that the best plan was to leave them there, as Spanish authorities were not hospitable to escapees that arrived from Vichy France. They also needed to rest, so the guide told them to stay where they were while he went to Barcelona. The guide contacted the British consul in Barcelona, and a representative soon arrived to pick Sale and his partner up. It was July 7 when he was brought to the British Consulate where he was kept until the final leg of his journey was arranged.

The arrangements were completed for Julian Sale to be moved to southern Spain, where he was able to make his way to British-held Gibraltar. Further arrangements were made to have Sale travel to England from Gibraltar. He arrived in Liverpool on August 10, which was about three months after he bailed out of his bomber. Sale had actually walked and bicycled about 800 miles to make the trek from Holland south to Spain. During that entire effort, Sale never came into contact with the organized French Resistance. Some have estimated that the trek to freedom by Sale was among the longest solo efforts of an escapee during World War II. The authorities were very quick to recognize the determination and effort that Sale had demonstrated in his escape from occupied Europe. In October 1943, it was announced that he would receive the Distinguished Service Order.

Julian Sale had not been in contact with any of the escape lines and knew nothing about their secret operations. He was in the unique position of being allowed to return to his squadron because he posed no threat of exposing secrets if he found himself behind enemy lines again and was arrested. Sale returned to No. 35 Squadron and was given a pathfinder role. The pathfinder was a bomber who had special training in navigation and target location for the night bombing raids. To pinpoint a target at night was difficult. The pathfinder would fly in front of the main bombing group and identify the target by dropping flares. The rest of the bombers in the group would focus on the flares, find the target and drop their bombs.

The period after Sale returned had some of the greatest action for bombers in World War II. He was soon promoted to squadron leader. On one occasion Sale was piloting a Halifax when it was hit, and there was a large fire aboard. Sale realized that a crewmember's parachute was badly burnt, and that if he bailed out, the crewmember was doomed. Sale returned to the pilot's seat to crash-land the bomber rather than abandoning his crewmember. For this extraordinary act of courage, he was awarded a bar for his Distinguished Service Order.

Sale was awarded the Distinguished Flying Cross for his bravery on the night of February 19, 1944. He was flying a Halifax as a pathfinder to target the city of Leipzig. During the operation, he was attacked by a German night-fighter. The Halifax suffered heavy damage and caught fire. During the attack Sale was badly wounded, but he held his course until his crew had bailed out. Despite his own wounds, he also bailed out. He survived the parachute jump but was unable to evade capture once he was on the ground. He received care, but he died of his wounds on March 20, 1944, in a German prisoner of war camp.

Flying Officer Gordon Biddle was flying with the RCAF 407 Squadron that was based in northeast Scotland in Wick. Biddle and his Canadian crew took off for a routine sortie around midnight on September 26, 1944, in their Wellington, with a crew of six. Their mission was to fly along the Norwegian coast to search for and attack German submarines that had surfaced to recharge their batteries at night. After a few hours of flying at 1000 feet while the crew searched for targets, there was an explosion in the starboard engine followed by a fire. Pilot Gordon Biddle and

George Death, the second pilot, worked quickly to extinguish the engine fire as the aircraft lost altitude. They realized immediately that they couldn't get the aircraft any higher. Biddle ordered the crew to eject all moveable equipment from the aircraft to make it lighter.

After they removed everything they could, the aircraft still did not climb. Biddle decided to dump enough fuel to lighten the load, keeping enough to complete the flight back to Scotland. George Death released the fuel from the tanks, but when he tried to shut the valve, he found that it was jammed open. The fuel drained away, and the plane was left with only 450 gallons in its reserve tank. Biddle knew that amount of fuel would only last for about 30 minutes of flight. Biddle had enough fuel to head into Norway and search for a good place to crash-land the Wellington.

About 6:00 AM Biddle turned the Wellington toward the mainland. As he approached a fjord, a small German convoy opened fire on the aircraft as it passed overhead. Biddle hoped to find a flat landing surface, but he saw only a rugged landscape below. Suddenly, the second engine stopped—the last of the fuel was used up. The pilot carefully dropped the plane down and cut through some electrical lines before coming to a stop in a field. The Wellington held together. The crew was unharmed in the landing and scrambled out of the aircraft.

The crew set fire to the bomber to reduce any chance of the Germans gaining information that they could use. They had landed in a militarized zone but found out that the watchtower overlooking their landing site had been abandoned the day before. The men recognized a nearby building as a schoolhouse. They were in a village on the west coast near Os, which was about 15 miles south of Bergen, Norway.

As the Canadians finished setting fire to the Wellington, Magnus Askvik, the schoolmaster, along with other civilians, approached the airmen. They told the crewmembers that the Germans were close and the men had only moments to get away. The civilians pointed in the direction the crew would have to travel to a safe refuge in a nearby fjord, a good hiding place for a short time until the Germans organized a search. Biddle and his men quickly walked in that direction, pulling off their tunics and turning them inside out to make it less obvious that they were airmen.

As they approached the fjord, they saw a group of four houses below and agreed that they had to contact the local people if they hoped to avoid capture. Airman Maurice Neil agreed to approach one of the houses. Moments after he knocked on the door and Ingeborg Bjornen answered, she was guiding them to a nearby cave. She had seen and heard the Wellington before it crash-landed. After the group was in the cave, which was surrounded by forest, Bjornen told them to stay there until she contacted her father and returned. They didn't have to wait too long before she came back with milk for them. At about 7:00 PM, she brought food and more milk for their supper. As they ate, she told them that the Resistance had made arrangements to move them to a much safer place. The crew felt relieved at the rapid response and the cooperation of the local people.

Bjornen told the Canadians that the leader of the local Resistance organization, Einar Evensen, saw their aircraft overhead and immediately hurried from the island where he lived towards the direction it had flown. He failed to find the crew, but when he arrived back at his home around midday, a message was waiting for him from Bjornen's father. Once he knew where the crew was hidden, he contacted his best men to prepare to move the airmen.

The men of the local Resistance knew that the Germans would carry out extensive searches of the mainland, so the best place for the Canadians to hide was on one of the nearby islands. The Norwegians chose the island of Strøno. They would have to move the aircrew on a boat at night right by German coastal posts, but the Resistance members thought they had a good chance of making it.

As evening approached, one of Bjornen's men arrived at the cave to guide the aircrew through a forested area to a small inlet. They waited until about 8:00 PM for a rowboat. They all climbed into the rowboat and rowed away in the darkness to another location where another boat was waiting. At this point, three of the aircrew moved from one boat to the other, and both boats started to row along the shore in the darkness. The aircrew noticed the oarlocks had been packed with sackcloth to muffle any sound of the rowing. They were lucky because it was an inky black night with a light wind that rustled the autumn leaves, muffling the sound of the rowboats in the water. The two boats slipped past a German patrol boat and under a bridge that was always guarded by German soldiers.

It was so dark that the aircrew were unable to see the faces of their rescuers until they pulled the boats onto the island and made their way up to a small hut. In the dim light, they saw their rescuers. Among them was Nils Røttingen, who had lived several years in the United States and spoke English. He told them that the Germans had done exactly what they all expected after the crashed Wellington was located, gathering all the local people and bringing them in for questioning. Nobody had told anything to the Germans.

The Norwegians then told Gordon Biddle and his crew that the leaders of the local Resistance—including Magnus Hauge and Jakob Hjelle, who was the head of the Resistance group at Deknings—had been contacted and were working on the airmen's escape. The plan for the next five days called for the Canadian aircrew to stay in the boathouse on the island at night where they would receive food and could sleep. Each day before dawn, the group would quickly slip out of the small building and go up into the wooded hills on the island to hide during the day. The Germans were determined to find the airmen and continued to sweep through the area each day. As the airmen stood in the hills of the island, they could watch the German patrol boat crews checking every possible hiding place and structure along the coast. As driven as the Germans were to find the Canadians, the Norwegians were just as intent on finding a way to evacuate the airmen to England.

Faced with such an intensive search by the Germans, the local Resistance members, including Helén Mowinkel-Nilsen, who had been trained by the Special Operations Executive (SOE) in England, agreed that the airmen had to be moved farther away from the area. The Resistance set a plan in motion to take the Canadians to Jakob Hjelle's group. The other group would take all of the men into the forested mountain region on the mainland. The airmen would be able to hide there until the search by the Germans ended.

On September 30, the Norwegians told the Canadians that the plan was in place. The Resistance members gave the airmen some civilian clothes and told them to be clean-shaven by the morning. The Canadians were ready at 10:00 AM when a motorboat arrived with Evensen and

Thorald Jacobsen. The aircrew climbed into the boat and hid under a tarpaulin, and the overloaded motorboat started its trip of about 15 miles to Lønningdal. They were about halfway through their journey when a German patrol boat appeared ahead of them, turned and headed toward the rescue boat. Evensen was the skipper on the small motorboat, and he held his course. The patrol boat continued until it was within approximately 200 yards, but when the Germans aboard were satisfied that the smaller boat was not hiding anything, they went on their own way.

With that same courage, the Norwegians took their small motorboat right past the German U-boat base at Hatvik and continued on to the agreed place at Lønningdal. Once ashore, Mowinkel-Nilsen and Hjelle took the Canadians to their community, where the villagers hid them and gave them new boots that they would later need. Soon, the group was on its way into the secluded mountains. In the forest, they arrived at a small wood building where they met two Norwegians who were evading the Germans. One was Haldor Øverdal, who the Gestapo wanted, and the second was Ivar Dyngelabnd, who had been the sheriff of Os. The Germans had identified him as being active against them. The two Norwegians welcomed the Canadians and helped provide security in the area to protect them all. The local Resistance had provided the men in the hut with cooking utensils and supplied food. The small building only had two beds and a loft, but there were a few benches and the floor that the men could also sleep on. They agreed to a rotation so that all of them could get a good rest during their stay. The group stayed together for one week.

Helén Mowinkel-Nilsen, an agent with the SOE, worked with a radio operator who had contact with England. She sent a message that the Canadian aircrew were safe. The message to England said that the Resistance had eight people safely in hiding, which caused those receiving the message to doubt that it was authentic. Mowinkel-Nilsen had to follow up with another message to verify what had been sent in the earlier transmission. The miscommunication caused a delay in preparing for the evacuation of the Canadians.

As soon as they understood the situation, the SOE started to work immediately on evacuating the Canadians. They prepared for a pickup of the aircrew using the famous "Shetland Bus" route. Using the British Broadcasting Corporation, the Norwegian Resistance received the coded message "Keep the meat cakes hot." The message meant that there would be a pickup for the aircrew at the islet Øspøy at the usual interval of two days after the message was broadcast. Øspøy was situated close to Austevoll, south of Bergen. This islet was a common meeting place where the Royal Norwegian Navy Special Unit staged evacuations. The Shetland Bus got its name because it was based in Scalloway, in the Shetland Islands.

By the time the Canadian airmen left the small building in the forest, it had been nicknamed "little Canada." The Canadians trekked out of their hiding place on October 8, 1944. The Norwegians gave them a meal to take with them. Soon they continued on their way to where a small boat waited for them. The group was taken to a secure beach close to Lønningdal, where Norwegians with automatic rifles were guarding potential places a German patrol could come from. Hjelle, who was on the beach waiting, had made the arrangements, including the guards. The operation was dangerous because the Canadians had to travel through a fjord that was swarming with German patrol boats, but the Norwegian crews were well trained and followed an exact timeline for the voyage. At about noon on the same day, Lars Orrebakken ran his boat, the *Snogg*, to the beach Hjelle directed him to. Once the boat came into the beach, the Canadians climbed on with Haldor Øverdal who brought along a Sten gun with five magazines to attack the Germans if needed.

As they made their way into the fjord, Orrebakken and Øverdal counted 15 German patrol boats. They waved greetings to those Germans who were watching them with binoculars. Despite the danger from the patrol boats, Gordon Biddle argued his boat should get closer to the U-boat berths at Hatvik. He expected to return in another Wellington to attack them soon and wanted more information. Øverdal refused to accept this argument and ordered Biddle to stay below the deck.

As they sailed away from Hatvik, the argument ended. The boat soon arrived at Austevoll, where the Canadians left the *Snogg* and made their way onto Sverre Østervoll's fishing boat, which was an integral part of the Shetland Bus operation. Once on board, the airmen had another three hours of sailing to get to the remote islet. It was a barren, windswept, cold place with a tiny hut on it. The Canadians would have to share the few beds and sleeping bags for two days until the Shetland Bus arrived. The Canadians received their food for the day each evening when Østervoll brought it on a small boat. No one had heard any information about the rescue ship. The Canadians asked Østervoll, by signing, if he had any way of finding out if the ship would come. Each time Østervoll would sign back that he had no information. They had no choice but to wait.

On the evening of the third day, October 11, 1944, Østervoll arrived and told them as well as he could without knowing English that the ship *Vigra* was on its way, commanded by the well-known captain Lief Larsen. The *Vigra* was a United States submarine chaser that had been modified for service as the Shetland Bus.

Lief Larsen arrived at Austevoll with supplies for the Norwegian Resistance and then came to a stop near the cliffs off shore to wait for the Canadians.

Østervoll hadn't been told that he was expected to have the Canadians waiting near the cliffs. The area Larsen was operating in was close to a German navel base, and there were heavy German patrols. Larsen was waiting without his anchor dropped in case he was discovered and had to make a run for it. Larsen was also told that if the Canadians were not in place for quick pickup, he was to immediately head back. But Larsen waited for four hours before he could make contact with those on shore. It took another two hours before Østervoll could get his boat to the islet, pick up the Canadians and return. Larsen waited the entire time, as he had done in the past. He also waited as the Canadians made use of a translator to thank Østervoll for all the help he had given them. Once the Canadians were aboard, Larsen slowly made his way out of the close islands in the area until he made it to open sea. Once in the open, he brought his speed to the maximum, and the Canadians were underway in rough conditions. The airmen arrived in Scotland on the morning of October 12, 1944.

The entire journey of the Canadian aircrew had taken 17 days. It was remarkable that they had crash-landed in one of Norway's most heavily German militarized zones, but with the help of large numbers of Norwegians, they had not been caught. The German patrols were almost immediately aware of the crash and survival of the crew. But, in spite of having to operate right under the occupying German forces and the extensive land, air and sea search, the six Canadians were taken from one place to the next and eventually to freedom by the Norwegian Resistance.

As it became clear to the Germans that the Norwegians had assisted the aircrew's escape, they reacted as they always did. Many locals were arrested, including Magnus Hauge. They were interrogated, tortured and imprisoned. Following World War II, many received honours for their sacrifices. When Lief Larsen was given the Distinguished Service Order for his many daring rescues and other operations as captain of the *Vigra*, the citation mentioned the rescue of Flying Officer Gordon Biddle and his crew.

Canadians pilots flying in the Middle East who found themselves caught behind enemy lines had to face a harsh desert climate, sometimes for weeks, before making it back to Allied lines. Many of the same principles applied to the men who were successful: the local population had to help when the escapees made contact with them; men successful at evasion also had to blend in or hide so the enemy wouldn't discover them. Added to these challenges was the need to ration food and water and to get to places that had wells. The escapees had to also travel through desert conditions every day because many crashed or bailed out of their aircraft hundreds of miles away from the Allied lines.

One outstanding story is that of officer Brian Johnston of the RCAF. Johnston was serving as the wireless operator with No. 70 Squadron, flying out of Abu Sueir, which was close to the Suez Cannel, in September 1942.

On the night of September 7, Sergeant R. Carter piloted a Wellington on a bombing sortie to Tobruk. The mission was uneventful until the Wellington made its final turn toward the target while flying at 12,000 feet six miles west of Tobruk. The bomber was hit by antiaircraft fire. The engines began to shake and the aircraft started to lose altitude fast. The crew moved quickly to release their bombs to reduce the weight. Moments after the bombs were away, both engines stopped. As Sergeant Carter worked to keep control of the engine, second pilot Sergeant Dennis Bebbington was successful in getting the starboard engine running again.

They had only a short time before they would have to crash-land, so they turned the Wellington southeast and flew into the desert. To keep the aircraft aloft as long as possible, the crew worked hard to throw out all the equipment they could. Johnston sent a SOS message to inform the base at Abu Sueir that they were going down and what their approximate location was. In a moment, Sergeant Carter turned the landing lights on to see the flat surface of the desert beneath the aircraft. The pilot brought the Wellington down for a relatively smooth landing. No one of the crew was injured as the bomber came to a stop.

Carter and Bebbington, the two pilots, told the other crewmembers that as they were landing, they saw some tracer fire nearby, which indicated that there were search parties operating in the region. When a bomber crash-landed behind enemy lines, the usual practice was for the crew to set it on fire to destroy anything the enemy could use. But because it was dark and such a fire would attract the search party directly to where they landed, they agreed not to set the Wellington on fire. The crew destroyed the wireless operator's codebooks, the radio and the bombsight.

Johnston was the only officer with the Wellington crew, so he took command of the escape operation. He had the crew collect all of the equipment and supplies they would need from the bomber. They took the navigator's compass and maps that showed the area out of the aircraft. The crew searched for all the emergency supplies, including a flare gun. Johnston had the crew gather as many containers as they could and put the water from the bomber into them. As the men prepared to start their journey across the desert, they drank the remaining water that was left over after the containers were full. The enemy was getting close, so as soon as they completed their preparations, they hurried away from the downed aircraft.

Soon after they started to walk, they realized that they had been forced to land farther south than they first thought, so they decided to head north to the coast. The airmen hoped that once they were on the coast, they would have a better chance of figuring out where they were.

The enemy was active in the northern regions, so they changed their plan again and soon found themselves at the crash site of the Wellington. After taking their bearings, they started another trek southeast to Bir Enba. The crew continued to walk until about 5:30 AM, when they decided to rest in a stand of scrub. They were still hidden in the scrub when the sun rose. The crew had no intention of travelling in the heat of the day. The men surveyed the land around them and saw a burnt-out truck that could provide shade, so they made their way to the truck and prepared to rest for the day. Johnston checked the emergency supplies and set out a plan for six days of rations for the crew.

As the daylight faded and cooler temperatures set in for the night, the aircrew gathered their supplies and continued their trek. They decided that the best direction would be straight south. The men marched through the night to travel as far as they could. As the sky became brighter, they saw another truck that was charred and blackened like the one they had stayed by the day before. The airmen made themselves comfortable for the heat of the day. Moments later, they watched as three Arabs arrived. The three invited the Canadians to come to a nearby encampment, where the people gave them a meal and some more food. The Arabs then took the airmen back to the truck to spend the rest of the day.

The crew continued their journey south the next day as the sun dipped to the horizon and darkness started to close in. The aircrew were on their way when they had the good luck of finding a water hole. They replenished their water before continuing their walk. The men made a second discovery that night—a track appeared in the darkness. It was the El Adem-Bir Sheferzen road, and they followed it to the southeast and continued along the next day. The road brought the group to the border between Libya and Egypt. There they found an abandoned, broken-down staff car that they used for shade the next day.

As they continued on their way during the evening, they came upon another group of Arabs who gave them water and food. The Arabs told them that they were not far from the small desert town of Bit-el-Khireigat. The aircrew continued on to the town, where they found more water to refill their bottles and stayed for an extra night and rest.

After they rested at Bit-el-Khireigat, Johnston and the crew of six from the Wellington continued walking toward Bir Enba during the night and resting during the heat of the day. Sergeant Davis played a leading role helping the crew make it through the trek. By the end of the third night,

Sergeant Croiseau, who was the rear gunner, had extremely painful blistered feet. The crew agreed to move north, where they were sure the main road ran in case they needed to surrender to get medical help.

On the 13th day of walking, they found a well. Sergeant Croiseau's feet were getting worse, so the crew agreed to rest and make a new plan. They decided that because they were close to the main road, they might be able to find a truck they could capture. Using the truck, they could drive on from where they were. Brian Johnston and Dennis Bebbington left the rest of the crew to rest while they walked toward the main road. They wanted to see how much traffic was on the road and whether there was a stopping place for vehicles nearby. The two found a hill they could walk up and watch the road at a distance. There was traffic moving. The pair returned to report that there might be a chance to capture a truck if they moved in closer and watched from the hill. The aircrew rested at the well during the day and waited for dusk. As the sun dipped lower, the group moved to the hill and had a meal as they waited for the darkness to come.

It was a moonlit night, so the men could walk toward the road and see much of the landscape around them. They took about an hour to make it to the road. The men continued up the road for what they thought was two miles when two trucks came into sight about a mile ahead. The crewmembers had found what they were looking for. They moved to the nearby hills and decided that Brian Johnston, R. Carter and Dennis Bebbington would approach the trucks with Sergeant Croiseau, the injured gunner. Croiseau had participated in ambushes during the Spanish Civil War and knew what to do. The other two airmen hid in the hills with the survival kit.

Johnston quickly approached the driver while the others moved to apprehend anyone in the back. The driver yelled to the men in the other truck as Johnston hit him. The occupants from the second truck responded quickly, so Johnston called out to the others to retreat as a gunfight started. Johnston and Carter made a quick run to the hills to get away, but Bebbington was already in the back of a truck, where he lost his hat. In the darkness, he was mistaken for an Italian soldier and was pressed into service with the others to find the attackers. With his bad feet, Croiseau was quickly captured. Johnston and Carter and two other aircrew ran into the desert away from the enemy.

Bebbington also ran away, using the darkness to escape. He realized that the others in his crew had no choice but to quickly escape into the desert to the south, so he continued in the same direction. Soon, he met an Arab who gave him water, and he filled his bottles. Bebbington was exhausted and stopped to sleep until the sun started to rise at the horizon. He decided to continue southward during the day in hopes of finding the rest of the aircrew. Eventually, he saw them in the distance, trekking south ahead of him. The lone airman quickened his paced and soon joined them. All the crew-members found out that Sergeant Croiseau had been captured that night. The enemy placed him in a prisoner of war camp. He was released when the war ended.

Things improved for the airmen as they trekked south because more frequently they began to meet groups of Arabs, who gave them food and water. One group of Arabs brought them to their camp and gave them a meal. Around midnight that same day, they were sent on their way to the southeast. The aircrew continued their trek for the 18th night when they came upon a herd of camels. As they passed, they saw the Arab who was herding the animals. The Arab man brought them to his village and gave them water. The Canadians rested there during the day and decided that regardless of the blisters on their feet and their many desert sores and insect bites, they would press on. The next night, they travelled about 20 miles.

They encountered another camp of Arabs at Ben Nasarra and decided to change direction that day. When night came, the men walked directly to the east. They had to climb down into dry riverbeds and out again, which made the walking much more difficult than they had expected, so they turned south again.

As they travelled south, they noticed that the sky was lit up with searchlights. After consulting their maps, they agreed it was the German air facility at Sidi Heneishi. The airmen decided to travel as quickly as they could to the south and then east to avoid any contact. The men were exhausted as the sun started to rise above the horizon. Following the often-repeated advice from the Arabs, they found a shaded place to rest during the day.

On day 24 of their trek, the airmen entered a village about 10 miles north of the Allied Fuka line. The villagers greeted the airmen in a friendly manner and gave them water and food, but the crewmembers could not find a single guide who would take them to the Allied forces. Johnston attempted to negotiate and made the offer of £100 for each crewmember who would be guided back to the Allied forces. No one in the village was interested.

With the intention of pushing as hard and fast as they could to return to Allied lines, Johnston led his men away from the village as night fell. They continued to walk with short breaks even as the sun rose and the day became hot. The men continued walking for the second day. Their water had nearly run out when they found themselves caught in an intense rainstorm. The airmen huddled in the extraordinary downfall and scrambled to retrieve their supplies, which got caught in a flood of water and gravel.

Early on day 27 of their journey, the airmen found themselves at the edge of the Quttara Depression. They continued to move southeast, skirting the salt marshes in the area. The men had been walking 18 hours continuously when they decided they had to stop for a rest. As they rested, a small group of Arabs arrived. They provided water and food for the men. For the price of all the money the Canadians had left, the Arabs provided a blanket. Once the airmen had rested and were ready to walk again, the Arabs guided them to Lake Magre. Later, when the leading Arab of this group was described, it was agreed that he was an agent that had been placed in the area by MI9.

At Lake Magre, the aircrew decided to rest—the men were exhausted and there was the shade of palm trees to protect them. They slept through the next night as well. The aircrew were awakened by the noise of jeeps in the area. Undercover, the group observed who had arrived. The airmen saw two Allied jeeps that were carrying members of the No. 4 South African Armoured Car Unit, so they quickly flagged the vehicles down and introduced themselves.

The airmen were taken to an oasis where the unit had a small base at Bir Nahid. The group had breakfast. Then the South Africans transported them to the unit headquarters on the other side of the front line. The airmen spent the night sleeping there. The next day, the crewmembers were transported to Seagull Camp in Alexandria, where they had a chance to rest.

The remarkable 29-day trek, led by 22-year-old Brian Johnston, was about 340 miles long. His story demonstrates how the assistance of the Arabs throughout the trek was crucial for the aircrew to get back to Allied forces. The airmen's determination to get back was also a key element.

There was no doubt that the men who had made the journey were worthy of recognition. Johnston was recommended for a Military Cross for his determination and leadership during the escape, but he was already recommended for a Distinguished Flying Cross (DFC) right before the last mission. The authorities decided to give him the DFC and added to the citation his outstanding leadership during the aircrew's escape and evasion in the Middle East.

Sergeant Bebbington and Sergeant Davis, the navigator on the mission, each received a military medal for their courageous contributions to the escape. Bebbington died in March 1943, when his bomber went missing during a sortie over the Mediterranean.

Canadian airmen made remarkable evasions and escapes from Greek islands that were occupied by the Germans during World War II. Greece entered the war on October 28, 1940, after Italian leader Benito Mussolini made it clear that he wanted to re-establish the Roman Empire. Mussolini had his ambassador to Greece, Emmanuele Grazzi, present Greek Prime Minister Ioannes Metaxas with an ultimatum demanding that Italian forces be given free passage across Greece. It was, in effect, a demand to surrender Greek sovereignty to Italian forces. The reply from the prime minister was clear and concise: no. Italian forces invaded from Albania and pushed into Greek territory, but they faced intense opposition because the Greek military had been preparing for such an offensive. The Greeks mounted a counterattack on November 14, 1940, which effectively pushed the Italians back to Albania. The Italians needed help from the Germans to successfully invade Greece on April 6, 1941.

After the occupation of Greece, a military bulletin in London showed that of all the occupied countries, Greece might be the most helpful to any Allied serviceman who was evading Germans or Italians. RCAF Flying Officer R. Adams and his crew of six proved this to be true.

The airmen were flying a Wellington on November 7, 1943. Adams took off at 8:00 PM from the airfield at Berka. The crew was searching in the area of Naxos, in the Aegean Sea, for signs of enemy shipping. They would attack any ships they found. The crew spotted a supply ship in the main harbour and prepared to attack. The Wellington descended to 60 feet above the water as it came on a direct attack, flying in from the south. Just as the aircraft was making its final approach, a sudden burst of antiaircraft fire threw the crew off and the bombs missed the ship.

Adams pulled away to check the situation in the aircraft. Everything was still operational, so he prepared for another attack half an hour later. The aircraft came in on the target as antiaircraft fire began again, but Adams held the course until Warrant Officer T. Faulkner, an Australian bomb aimer, got the bombs away. The crew watched and were absolutely sure the bombs hit the target.

This time it was clear that the antiaircraft fire had damaged the Wellington. Adams and his second pilot, Flying Officer John Spencer, worked together to turn the aircraft in a direction that would take them over the Aegean Sea. The starboard engine and wing were badly damaged, and the crew was not sure if the engine would continue to run. The pilots struggled to gain as much altitude as they could, but the climb levelled off when the engine stopped. Almost as soon as they levelled out, the aircraft began to descend toward the water below. It was clear that they were not going to be able to make it back to the Berka airfield. Adams turned the Wellington into the wind and began to ditch the aircraft into the sea. The men were lucky that night because the surface of the water was completely calm. The Wellington came down smoothly, and the crew was uninjured.

The crew quickly inflated the dinghy. As the aircraft slowly started to sink, the men climbed into the dinghy and paddled away from the wreck. They were lucky in where they landed, as there was no question about which direction they would paddle—there was an island not too far away. Shortly after midnight, the crew was able to pull their boat onto the shore of Sifnos. The crew took all of the supplies out of the dinghy and destroyed it. They made their way to the wall that was along the shore and slipped into a hiding place. They men rested there until the sun rose.

The members of Adams crew had not yet stepped out of their hiding place in the morning when a young girl walked by and saw them. She motioned for them to follow her, which they did. Soon, they met her father—her family lived close to where the men had landed on the shore. The crewmembers told the man who they were. He told the aircrew that there were no Germans on the island at the time and that there was a small town near the centre of the island. The airmen were soon on their way to find help. The walk to the town took them until sometime in the afternoon. Once they identified themselves to the locals, they were taken into a house and treated well with a meal. The crew remained in the small town while word spread of their arrival. Late in the afternoon, a man who spoke English presented himself. He invited them to spend some time at his house on the outer rim of the community.

The man then took the crew to be introduced to the chief of police and the local priest.

Together, the leading men of the town decided that the safest place for the aircrew was at the local monastery. The priest took the men to the monastery, where they received exceptional hospitality.

The islanders sent word to the chief of police on the nearby island of Serifos. He arranged for the aircrew to be placed on a caique, a local type of boat, which brought them to his island. There was a problem with the arrangements because the airmen had been in the small town monastery for three days and the entire population of the island knew they were there. Many of the Greeks stopped by to visit. The first boat operator refused to take the airmen to the nearby island because a large crowd wanted to give the men a public farewell. Germans were on a nearby island, and the boat operator was fearful they would find out he had helped the men. The result was that the aircrew waited two more days and their departure was set for 6:00 AM with a different boat. The other boatman was also fearful when he took the men to Serifos and decided to avoid the obvious landing site on the north shore, taking them to the southern coast instead. The aircrew had to walk around the island to the north.

The men started to walk, but they decided to make themselves comfortable for a night in the open. The next day they started their trek across the island to where they would contact the chief of police and hide in another monastery. They were supposed to make contact with the priest before anyone else in the community, but as they walked across the island, the aircrew met local citizens who were happy to help them, giving them food, water and directions to the monastery. When the crew of the Wellington arrived at the monastery, members of the British Long Range Desert Group (LRDG), who had been carrying out secret operations in the area, met them. Lieutenant Gibson led the LRDG. They were finished their work and had to be transported off the island as well. The aircrew led by Adams joined the LRDG members because they would have to wait for the arrangements to be made for a ship. The wait lasted for three weeks while the servicemen stayed in a series of different caves scattered across the island.

After several delays, Adams and his crew got ready to be picked up on November 25, 1943, by a bigger motorized caique. The Royal Navy operated the boat as a part of the Levant Schooner Flotilla. The boat was based in Beirut and had duties that included support for LRDG operations in the Greek Islands and mainland. The boat also carried out intelligence gathering in the Aegean Sea. Because of all these activities and bad weather, the boat was delayed. The aircrew and the members of the LRDG had their own supplies of food and water that had been cached on the island for Allied operations, but when the Royal Navy caique did not arrive, the supplies ran out. The men radioed their situation to the captain of the boat, and an effort was made to drop more supplies from air, but the bad weather kept the drop from happening. The local population stepped in and gave the servicemen the supplies they needed.

In the darkness, shortly after midnight, the *Levant Schooner 2*, captained by Lieutenant Alexander McLeod, arrived at Serifos. McLeod took a rowboat to the shore, where Adams and Gibson met him. With the unpredictable weather, there was a sense of urgency as they prepared to load the 12 men aboard the *Levant Schooner 2* and leave. The arrangements were not complete when the weather suddenly turned bad. McLeod quickly moved the schooner to a hiding place where the crew worked to put up camouflage. They waited for better weather.

The weather was more cooperative the next day, and the *Levant Schooner 2* left at about 6:15 PM. The schooner headed to the island Iraklia. The ship made it there as the sun was rising, and McLeod anchored at the side of a rocky cliff where the camouflage was set. He had instructions to wait at this place to pick up two more RAF airmen and a LRDG agent. As the day wore on, it became clear that the three men were not going to arrive. McLeod had to move on without them. The next place they planned to sail to was a base close to

Turkey where they could get more supplies. They were running low on rations and fuel.

As the sun moved toward the horizon and darkness fell on the schooner, the crew was busy getting underway. They were sailing east for about three hours when the motors began to break down. There was no way of knowing how long they would be able to travel with this trouble, so McLeod changed the course toward Anidros. They set anchor and the crewmen set to work to repair the engines as fast as they could. As the engine was repaired, McLeod headed across the island to gather what information he could about what was happening.

The crew had the schooner's engines working, but there were more problems. They headed out to sea in an eastward direction, but because they were moving slowly with frequent breakdowns, they had to stop to hide by the island of Sirina. While they were there, McLeod set to work giving the civilians food and other supplies in compensation for the assistance they gave the aircrew. The local population hid the aircrew and provided food and water to them.

Once it was dark, the *Levant Schooner 2* continued in the same slow manner to the island of Loryma, where they needed to pick up supplies from a cache. The crew got the ship to the island after midnight on December 3, 1943. The crewmen loaded 50 gallons of fuel, and then they were able to sail to the islands along the Turkish coast in Turkey's territorial waters on their way to Castelrosso. The ship moved on to Port Vathy because it had to meet a Special Boat Squadron for supplies in the morning of December 5.

McLeod had his crew sail the schooner during the day along the coast of Turkey until darkness fell. The schooner turned out to sea and headed for Cyprus. The ship arrived in the harbour of Paphos about noon. Adams and the Wellington aircrew stepped ashore for debriefing. Soon, they were on a flight back to Cairo where they were interviewed by the Air Headquarters staff.

The Greek people played a central role in the escape of Adams's crew. As the war continued, the Greeks continued to resist the occupation by the Germans and the Italians. The Resistance in Greece continued with vigorous campaigns in spite of German retaliation. The Greeks worked with the Special Operations Executive (SOE) agents to sabotage German efforts and to carry out actions such as blowing up bridges, which separated German troops from their supplies.

CHAPTER SEVEN

The Canadian Spy
Who Escaped

FOR CANADIANS WORKING FOR THE SPECIAL OPERATIONS Executive (SOE) behind enemy lines, there was only one option when the Gestapo found out about their work and started to hunt them down: they had to escape from occupied countries. When the Germans found an SOE agent, man or woman, who had been trained in sabotage and spying, he or she was arrested, interrogated, tortured and executed. Unlike aircrew, soldiers or sailors on the run in occupied countries—who would be interrogated and sent to prisoner of war camps—agents faced execution. Other agents who worked for the SOE worked with MI9 to quickly move discovered spies into hiding and back to England. One such story is that of Canadian SOE agent Joseph Gabrielle Chartrand, who was operating in occupied France when he was discovered.

Joseph Gabrielle Chartrand joined the Royal Montreal Regiment and arrived in England in December 1939. He was capable and intelligent but too old to be trained as an infantry officer because he was 32. Because of his fluency in English and French, he was transferred to a clerk's position at the Canadian Military Headquarters in London and worked at the Judge Advocate's branch.

The situation began to change when Chartrand had a discussion with his older brother Paul, who was serving with the Régiment de Maisonneuve stationed in southern England. Paul told Joseph that their old friend from Montréal, Gustave Daniel Bieler, was in the same regiment and they should meet. Joseph and Gustave spent time together with Joseph's fiancé in their small residence in Bramham Gardens in Kensington.

By the middle of 1942, Chartrand moved again to a position as a statistics clerk. He was increasingly unhappy and wanted to find something else to do. Bieler saw how miserable his old friend was and suggested that he could help by recommending him to the people he worked for. Chartrand agreed immediately, but Bieler cautioned him that it would be a strange experience. Bieler warned the 32-year-old Canadian to expect a bizarre interview to start the process. Chartrand was still interested and asked Bieler to go ahead.

Joseph Chartrand was soon called to a hotel room to meet with some men, and the meeting was as strange as his friend suggested it would be. Chartrand entered a hotel room that had been completely emptied of all furnishings except a table and three chairs. Two men dressed in civilian clothes conducted the interview. The questions appeared to have no focus, and they gave no information about what service Chartrand might be involved in. At the end of the interview, one of the men presented him with a piece of paper with an address on it. Chartrand was told to read and remember the address but not to write it down. The interview was over when they told Chartrand to arrive at that address on Monday at 10:00 AM.

Chartrand went to the offices of the SOE on Baker Street to continue the discussion. After the introductions were over, Chartrand was asked to join the SOE, and he accepted. He was soon in the training program to become an agent. He found out that his old friend Bieler had the best reputation among all the agents in the service. Chartrand learned how to sabotage factories and equipment. He also trained vigorously in making his escape when being pursued by police or other service personnel, and he learned to parachute.

With his training complete, Chartrand was on his way to occupied France on April 14, 1943. He travelled with a journalist who had no training in parachuting, so they flew in one of two Lysanders that landed in a meadow right by the walls of Amboise. Four passengers arrived that night. The French Resistance misunderstood the message that had been sent. They brought only two bicycles for the four men and had made no arrangements for the agents' suitcases.

The four agents set out for a railway station 11 miles away. Charles Liewer, one of the agents, and Chartrand agreed to walk to the station. The two hurried along to the station and took a train to Tours, where they arrived at a safe house established by the French Resistance at the École Supérieure pour Jeunes Filles de Tours. However, a surprise visit from the German authorities to check that the school was using approved textbooks forced Liewer and Chartrand to be rushed away moments before the inspectors arrived, saving them from arrest.

Chartrand was quickly moved to a safe house in Tours, where he stayed for two weeks. At the same time, Liewer quickly made his way to Rouen where he had plans to establish a new group of saboteurs.

Liewer and Chartrand were on the move during Holy Week and travelled through Paris, where they seemed to be unable to escape close contact with German soldiers. They were sitting side by side with them at Mass, on city buses and at the bistros. They rubbed shoulders when they walked down the street. Liewer, who knew the city well, guided Chartrand. Chartrand had made other friends in Liewer's two half brothers, who were members of the French Resistance.

Joseph Chartrand used the identity of a life insurance salesman, which was convenient because salesmen need to travel. He had the added security of having the switchboard operator at a Paris-based insurance company confirm that he worked for the company, if anyone phoned to ask. But there were some problems with Chartrand's cover, which included the Germans' recent discovery that SOE agents were routinely given such identities. The cover worked so well that it was overused by the SOE. The Germans' knowledge would not have been a significant problem except that Chartrand was out past the curfew in Rouen one night. The Germans had imposed a regulation that absolutely every person who was detained by the police had to be reported to the German authorities. The Germans were carefully searching for all life insurance salesmen, and there was ongoing intense security by the Germans in Rouen because it was close to the English Channel. Luckily, the local police shared this information with Liewer.

Chartrand and Liewer had to move quickly because it was clear that the Germans would gain specific information about Chartrand. In the case of Joseph Chartrand, the SOE had allowed him to keep his own name on his papers. Chartrand had to change his identity and move from Rouen to a place with far fewer Germans.

François Garel, who was with the Department of the Sarthe, which was a division of the région Pays-de-la-Loire, and a member of the SOE, arranged the transfer. He was organizing the Butler circuit and knew Liewer. Joseph Chartrand became

Claude Carton, an inspector of pensions. He travelled to Château-du-Loir, about 25 miles from Tours.

While Chartrand was in the Château-du-Loir and Tours area, he helped François Garel establish the Butler circuit during June 1943. The initial aim of the circuit was to take out the rail lines around Angers. Chartrand was busy finding and training recruits for the French Resistance. There were numerous drops of supplies, and the new recruits had to be trained in the use of Sten guns. The operations were completed with the destruction of the railroad lines. But Chartrand was aware that there was generally weak security in the circuit. Garel enjoyed a good social life, and the general consensus was that he drank too much for a SOE agent. Chartrand's concerns were vindicated on September 7, 1943, when François Garel, his mistress and the radio operator for the Butler circuit were all arrested in Paris.

There had been more sophisticated efforts on the part of the SOE to increase the security of its agents in occupied France, but the Germans had also demonstrated an improved ability to find secret agents. The Butler circuit had been associated with the Prosper circuit, which also had bad security. The members of the Prosper circuit had a poor understanding of how secrecy had to work on the line. But the main reason for the downfall of the Butler line was that the Germans had picked up one of the circuit's sub-agents in a routine security check. The agent had told the Germans everything they wanted to know before he was sent to the prisoner of war camp in Ravitsch, Poland.

Garel was interrogated and imprisoned at Buchenwald, where he was executed. Chartrand felt lucky that he had not been arrested at the same time and moved quickly to find a hiding place. He destroyed his identity papers and became George Chenier, a clothing salesman. With his new identity papers, Chartrand assisted the French Resistance in moving an American airman from Missouri to a safe house in the countryside by Tours. He then headed back to Tours on his bicycle, but he ran into two Gestapo agents who demanded that he get off his bicycle at gunpoint. He did as he was told and dismounted. Then he was told to let the air out of the tires of his bicycle.

As Chartrand listened to the air hissing out of the tires, he remembered his training. The first moments of arrest were one of the last chances for escape. Once you entered the police building and they closed the cell doors, it was all over. Interrogation, torture and imprisonment would follow. Once you were in prison, execution was inevitable. The Gestapo agents told him to push his bicycle as they marched him toward their headquarters. They had plans for the bicycle, but it would provide him with what he needed to make his getaway. He knew that if he could just get 15 good long strides of a run, he could make his getaway. One of the Gestapo stopped and ordered the other to escort Chartrand the rest of the way to the police station. The Gestapo agent hurried down a side street. Chartrand saw that the police headquarters was about 900 feet away. His bicycle was on his left, and there was a street to the left. The Gestapo agent was too relaxed as Chartrand suddenly pulled the bicycle off the ground and threw it at him. The surprised Gestapo officer was thrown off balance. By the time he was able to push the bicycle away and aim his pistol at the fleeing Chartrand, it was already too late. Bullets flew by Chartrand as he disappeared down the street. He darted from street to street as fast as he could to put as much distance as possible between himself and the Gestapo officer.

Joseph Chartrand was safe from the Germans for the moment, but he knew that he was well known to them. He quickly discovered the traitor who had brought about the destruction of the Butler circuit. He telephoned the apartment of Garel's mistress, and a man with a thick German accent answered the phone. Chartrand knew he was in grave danger because the Germans knew all of his identities up to that point and had a clear idea of who he was. He had to hide and find a way to escape. It was difficult as he made his way around Paris. He had no money, and he was not in contact with any of the other agents he had known.

As Joseph Chartrand was walking along the Champs Elysées, he began to doubt that he would make it out of France. He looked around and was astonished to see his old friend Charles Liewer. In moments, Liewer knew that he had to get his old friend out of France as directly as possible. Liewer took Chartrand to a safe house. Shortly after, he sent a message to the authorities in London telling them what had happened. Late in autumn, Chartrand was moved to another apartment in Paris. He met a Royal Australian Air Force (RAAF) squadron leader who he helped by moving him along an escape line.

Shortly after the RAAF airman was on his way, Chartrand was taken into an escape line by an agent code-named Paul, who was Irving Dent, a Viennese Jew. Under his old identity papers as George Chenier, Chartrand travelled to Rennes, where he met two French Resistance agents and a United States Air Force gunner. They waited for an all-clear message before they moved on to Brittany. The plan called for the escapees to be picked up at night on a beach on the Brittany coast by a Royal Navy gunboat. The entire operation had to be organized in the heavily guarded and occupied coastal area. The Germans continued to carefully guard the coast in preparation for the expected invasion. As the years passed, the Germans built up their presence in Brittany and Normandy. At the same time, those who were organizing escapes found the established lines too long and time consuming. The need for a route that would take those being evacuated from France straight across the English Channel was increasing because of the growing numbers of aircrew who were bailing out or crash-landing in the occupied countries.

The group of escapees moved from the safe house at Rennes to an old flourmill in Normandy, about 19 miles from the beach they would escape from. The mill was not in use because it was broken down. The men maintained a cover as workmen who were restoring the mill to operation. They prepared to move from the flourmill to the beach, which was guarded and close to German positions. The night came for the evacuation, and the men arrived at the beach in darkness.

The days when escape operations could be carried out were carefully coordinated. The tides had to be just right, and there had to be no moon at all. The operation would have to be carried out in pitch-blackness. Those who arrived for the pickup had to follow a carefully established process so that they would all be able to make their way down the rocky cliffs to the beach.

The escapees had exact orders how to follow each other down to the beach. They carefully descended the cliff until they were partway down. The sky was bright with flares. The signal told everyone that something had gone wrong—they would have to move quickly and silently back to the top of the cliff. The group rushed back to Rennes to hide until the conditions were right for another attempt.

The conditions were good again on December 9, 1943, so the men moved to the coast. The evacuees were cold and nervous during their second attempt to escape from the dangerous Brittany coast. They knew the routine and made their way down onto the beach. On the beach, they sat down in the inky darkness of the night. The group waited in silence, listening intently for the sound of the Royal Navy gunboat. They watched as one of their guides sent a signal out to sea using a flashlight and the flashes of another light came back. There was a feeling of anticipation as they waited. They could hear the quiet splash of oars. Out of the darkness of the sea, a rubber dinghy came into view and landed on the beach. It was heavy with supplies that were quickly unloaded onto the beach. Several new agents got out of the dinghy and helped move the supplies. In what felt like mere moments, Chartrand was sitting down in the rubber dinghy. He felt the gentle pull of the oars and the push of the men on the beach. The shore faded in the darkness, but Chartrand didn't start to relax until he was on the Royal Navy gunboat

There was no chance for Chartrand to change from the dirty black pants and the black woman's sweater he arrived at the beach wearing. He had given his clothes to the French Resistance because the supply of civilian clothing was stretched to its limit.

Chartrand was interviewed by the SOE, and it was agreed that under no condition could he be sent back to occupied France. The Germans had far too many details about him. To send him back would be suicidal.

After France was liberated, Chartrand did return to act as a censor for the press and radio in Paris. Later, he became a censor in Brussels.

Joseph Chartrand's escape from occupied France was the result of his own resolve, his quick-minded efforts, the assistance of other SOE agents and members of the French Resistance, and the existing escape line to the Brittany coast.

CHAPTER EIGHT

Escaping Italian Camps

IN ITALY THERE WAS LITTLE ENTHUSIASM FOR THE WAR, especially after Benito Mussolini attempted to create a North African Roman Empire. With this effort, the Italian army suffered massive casualties. The Allies defeated the Italian forces on all fronts.

As the war continued in North Africa, the Germans brought large numbers of prisoners to Italian prison camps. The majority of these prisoners were Indians, Australians, British and New Zealanders, but among them were a small number of Canadians. The majority of these prisoners were airmen who had been shot down behind enemy lines.

The morale of the prisoners in the Italian prison camps increased after they received news of the surrender of the German Afrika Korps on May 13, 1943, ending the North Africa campaign with an Allied victory. The prisoners expected an invasion of Italy. This expectation was fulfilled in July when Sicily was invaded by British, American and Canadian troops. After a little more than a month, Sicily fell to the Allies. The tide had turned against

Italy, and Benito Mussolini resigned on July 25, 1943. He was immediately arrested.

The invasion of the Italian mainland came on September 3, 1943. The success of the Allied forces and the Italian populace's opposition to the war brought the country's surrender on September 8. The surrender of Italy was not a surprise to anyone, including the Germans.

Pietro Badoglio became the leader of Italy after Mussolini resigned. Badoglio declared martial law as he pursued a peace treaty with the Allies. German forces occupied Rome and attained the capitulation of Italian forces that were in northern Italy. These events permitted a rapid mass breakout at the Italian prisoner of war camps after the terms of the armistice between Italy and the Allies were published on September 8, 1943. The Germans rushed south to restore the prison camps and capture those who had escaped. Many prisoners moved southward as quickly as they could to meet up with the advancing Allied armies. Swift action by the Germans meant many of those who escaped were recaptured.

❧✦❧

Flight Sergeant Bill Oxendale was in the prisoner camp P.G. 59 at Sevigliano after he was shot down on February 25, 1942. Oxendale was a pilot in Ferry Command who was flying a Wellington bomber to the Middle East that day, but he never made it.

When the Italian forces capitulated, Oxendale and his prison mates were overjoyed. They realized that they had a chance to break out before the inevitable arrival of German troops. Soon, they heard that the Germans were only 20 miles away from Ascoli. At the same time, stories were circulating among the Italian guards that the Germans were shooting Italians on sight. The result was a mass desertion as the Italians wanted to run as much as the prisoners. There were reports of the guards appearing on patrol with rifles and suitcases.

The guards told the prisoners that if the Germans continued to advance toward the camp, the guards would release the prisoners that night. As the night fell on the camp, general confusion reigned because some guards were not sure what they should do. However, some prisoners were released. Under a full moon, they made their run for freedom. Some guards responded to the mass movement of prisoners by shooting into the air, but that did not slow the rush of prisoners out of the camp in a southward direction.

Oxendale was with a group of 12 others who went to higher land, where they stayed in a farmer's house. They found out that an armed column of Germans was in the valley immediately below the house. The men moved on and stayed at the small village of San Giovanni, about 10 miles from the camp. They stayed there for a week.

The group had decided to split up and move on from the village when a local woman ran through the streets yelling "Tedske!" which meant that the Germans were coming into the village. The men heard shots as they rushed south. The Germans had discovered that a ravine near the village had several hundred prisoners occupying it.

Just before they heard the shots, Oxendale was discussing whether he and his groups should leave the village. A British sergeant major was arguing that he wanted to stay because he had sciatica, which made it difficult to walk. The sound of the shots ended the conversation, and they began to run. The sergeant major outran the others in his group. As they quickly moved southward and into the mountains, they met up with some of those who had been in the ravine. The group had quickly scattered when the Germans moved in.

As the men moved toward Ascoli, Oxendale's group noticed that there were increasing numbers of German patrols. To avoid running into the Germans, the groups would have to be extra careful. The escapees decided to split up, with one part moving ahead to scout the road they were on. The lead group moved around a bend in the road and ran into a patrol of Germans. The scouting men were captured and taken to a prisoner of war camp in Germany. Oxendale's group, which had brought up the rear, took cover and avoided the same fate.

Oxendale and his companions pushed on more carefully, moving at one point upstream in a brook to confuse the dogs that were following. As they moved, Oxendale noticed a German transport.

Oxendale and his group made their way along a narrow mountain path, but they turned a blind corner and were suddenly among Germans who were manning a 105-millimetre gun. After a long journey that had taken two months, the escapees were devastated to be captured again.

After a stop at a monastery for one night, Oxendale was taken to Chieti, which had been a British officers' prisoner of war camp. He had only been in the camp a few hours when he found that some prisoners had been digging an escape tunnel. The officers who had been at the camp before the capitulation of the Italian forces had begun the tunnel. The Germans had arrived to take over the camp, but they had not discovered the underground passage. It was complete, and that night there was going to be an escape. The prisoners showed Oxendale the entrance behind the stove in the cookhouse as plans went ahead.

The tunnel was dug with a U shape at the bottom of the entrance. It was late in November, and the escapees would have to contend with icy cold water that had filled the U. The tunnel came out just under the wall, where the escapees could push themselves through a hole that had been cut in the barbed wire.

Oxendale and four other men made their way through the tunnel at night. Once the men were clear of the tunnel, the full moon made it possible to move more easily. They looked around and crawled for about 50 feet from the hole in the wire to a forested area. After their previous experience evading the Germans, the group agreed to split up, staying close enough to know where each other was, but not walking as a group. They made their way along the low-lying areas because the Germans were known to take the high ground to watch as much territory as possible. The greatest danger was from walking right into them.

Oxendale's group was lucky. They made their way south until they were nearly at the Sangro River. The river was close to the front line of the invading forces. The group stayed in the area while the invasion continued. After two weeks, the Allied forces increased the intensity of their attack when American bombers dropped their loads on German positions.

The morning after the bombings began, Oxendale and his fellow escapees decided to run for the Allied lines because they were too close to the German positions. As soon as they got on their way, an Italian boy approached them and called out for them to follow him. They were not sure if they should follow but decided to do so. The escapees entered a house and met some advanced scouts from the Second New Zealand Division.

The group stayed in the house until around 4:00 PM when a jeep took them back behind the Allied lines. Moments after they left the house, a German counterattack was launched and the Germans captured the area.

The group made their way south to Bari by hitchhiking. At Bari, the group boarded a troop ship to travel to Sicily and across to Bizerte in North Africa. Bill Oxendale's group was with about 100 escapees who travelled to Algiers where they boarded the *Louis Pasteur* on January 2, 1944. Bill and his group went to the Canadian repatriation centre at Warrington. They travelled to London for four days of debriefing and left for Canada on January 27.

❧❖❧

After being shot down in the desert of North Africa on October 19, 1942, Pilot Officer Ed Patrick found himself at P.G. 78 prison camp at Sulmona. When the Italians capitulated to Allied forces, Patrick heard that prisoners of war had been instructed to remain where they were. But the Italians in his camp decided that they would leave. Reports of the rapid movement of German troops were one of the reasons for quick action. No one in the camp trusted that the Germans would leave them where they were. Many prisoners were sure they would be moved to prisoner of war camps in Germany.

Those who were in the prisoner of war camps knew that many rural Italians were anti-Tedske, which meant anti-German. The escapees knew they would get help from the local people as the prisoners made their way south to join the invading Allied forces.

In September 1943, a large group of prisoners marched to the height of a nearby hill. As they set up camp for the night, they found German troops among them capturing a number of the men. The escapees scattered before they could be taken as well. Some, like Patrick, hid in nearby leaves or the brush. They came out of their hiding places as soon as the Germans moved from the area. A group of six escapees moved down the other side of the hill the next morning.

As the men walked to San Vittorino, a nearby village, Ed Patrick twisted his ankle. The local people, who did not support the fascist forces, quickly took the group in. Patrick needed time for his ankle to recover. The Orsini family provided a hiding place for a week. Patrick was comfortable in the Orsinis' care. He, like other Allied personnel, had been instructed to stay with rural people if he escaped because rural Italians were usually anti-fascist and anti-Tedske. They would provide assistance even though it was known that they would be shot if they were found harbouring escapees or evaders.

After the week had passed, only two escapees were left in the village—Ed Patrick and Flight Lieutenant Gilbert "Mickey" Middlemass, who was captured after a bombing raid on Turin on November 17, 1942. In the raid, his Pathfinder had to find the target ahead of the rest of the bombers and drop flares for them. Once his plane was over the target, the flares were released, but one continued to burn in the bomb bay. Everyone on board thought that the Pathfinder was on fire, so the rest of the five crewmembers bailed out. The pilot was preparing to jump when he realized that the flare had burned out and the plane was not on fire. The pilot made his way back to the cockpit and returned to England alone.

Patrick and Middlemass worked their way south carefully, making their way across three rivers. They were constantly careful of where the Germans were. The two men took about 40 days to reach freedom. They knew that the German front line was not heavily guarded and was always changing with various groups changing positions. The two waited in cover until they saw an opening and then rushed through the line.

As they moved forward, they walked around a bend and came into the full view of two soldiers with automatic rifles. Fearing that they would be shot, Patrick and Middlemass immediately threw their hands up. The soldiers motioned the two to follow them. Patrick relaxed when he saw

"Canadian" on one of their uniforms. They found out that these two scouts were from the Royal 22nd Regiment. The regiment's scouts had a reputation of shooting first and asking questions later.

The two men were taken to the scouts' captain who then brought them to the intelligence officer. Both men were interrogated to make sure they were who they said they were. Soon they were enjoying a meal, a shave and a bath.

Flying Officer Raymond John Fredrick Sherk from Hamilton, Ontario, enlisted on September 16, 1940. He was stationed with No. 601 Squadron as a part of the African contingent. Flying an Mk IX Spitfire, Sherk flew with a three-aircraft formation under orders to find and destroy an ammunition train in the area of Charing Cross, near Marsa Matruth, Egypt, in September 1942.

As they flew in low, they did not find the ammunition train. The pilots turned back because they were running low on fuel. Suddenly, from above, three Junkers 52s, bombers with two engines, attacked the formation. The three Allied aircraft rapidly manoeuvred around the Junkers and shot one down while the others retreated. As the Allied formation continued back to its base, Sherk switched from his long-range tanks to his regular tanks, but an airlock interrupted the fuel supply and the engine stopped. Flying at 200 feet, he did not have time to recover and had to set the Spitfire down. Sherk radioed his position to his leader, who ordered him to leave the aircraft behind and make his way to the Allied lines on foot. The pilot took his escape kit and rations and started to walk. As the sun rose, he hid and slept as he waited for night to continue on his way.

As Flying Officer Sherk approached the Allied lines in the dark in the last week of September 1942, an Italian patrol caught him. The patrol took him to a nearby camp where the officer in charge interrogated him. Sherk was searched and had all of his things taken away. He gave his required name, rank and service number. Luckily, the officer gave Sherk his pack of cigarettes back. Sherk had previously hidden a compass in the package. The Canadian was taken to the Italian headquarters where he found that the intelligence officer spoke English well but was not as easygoing as the first officer. Sherk shared nothing with the Italian, who had Sherk's uniform taken away and made him wear a German flying suit. He was sent out to sleep in the sand by the camp's two guards. When the guards fell asleep, Sherk rushed into the night, but he only made it about 90 feet before they were in pursuit. Sherk realized that he might be shot and decided to pretend he was simply relieving himself.

The next morning he was taken to El Daba, where there was a military facility, including an airfield. His guards were ordered to hitchhike with him to a location farther along. When the group was unable to get a ride, Sherk was jailed in El Daba for the night. In the morning, Sherk was handed over to the Germans and placed in a tent. A man who was dressed as a Red Cross official and spoke English arrived to hand him a series of forms with questions that were like those asked by the interrogators. Sherk filled in his name, rank and service number and handed it back to the man. The man looked at the form and then produced a series of forms that were filled out in full. He demanded that Sherk do the same. Sherk looked at the names, but he did not recognize any of them, although he would not have filled out his own form if he had. He refused to divulge anything. The official became annoyed and ordered that Sherk be stripped and searched. The guards then marched him to a tent where he remained naked for several days.

The interrogation tactics changed on October 3, 1942, when the Germans pointed out that Sherk was wearing a German flying suit and accused him of being a spy. Sherk refused to give any information, but he realized that the interrogator's rage was too intense. He volunteered false information, saying that he was with the No. 74 Squadron. He stated that he had been flying a Spitfire that was shot down on September 26.

The interrogator was satisfied. He gave Sherk his clothes back and sent him to a tent where another prisoner was being held. The prisoner was a South African whose story of being an air observer who was shot down in a Halifax bomber was suspicious. He insisted that Sherk cooperate with the Germans, but Sherk told him nothing.

Within days, Sherk was sent back to the Italians. He found himself in a tent with another prisoner who said he was a pilot from Southend-on-Sea in England. The man was able to correctly tell Sherk who his commander was, so Sherk confided that he had been able to keep his compass hidden in his pack of cigarettes. Sherk also told him that he had been with the No. 601 Squadron and that he had been picked up a day after he made a forced landing. Sherk realized later that day that the prisoner he had been talking to was an agent for the Germans. The Canadian was handed back to the Germans, and his compass was taken from his pack of cigarettes.

Ray Sherk was placed with two British prisoners in a tent at Mersa on October 6, 1942. Both of them had stories like Sherk's about the prisoner who was supposed to be from Southend-on-Sea. Clearly the man from Southend was just another German agent. The next day, Sherk joined a larger group that was transferred to Derna, on the Libyan coast, and then taken to Lecee. The Germans put the group on a train the next day and took them to Bari, Italy, where Sherk was in solitary confinement for three weeks. Once he entered the main camp, he was astonished to see the terrible conditions and the starving prisoners.

The conditions in the camp did not improve until February 1943, when the prisoners received new clothes and Red Cross parcels began arriving. The parcels provided the prisoners with food, tea, coffee, cigarettes and so on.

Sherk moved again on March 3, 1943, to the Sulmona camp where conditions were better. Sherk wasted no time in agreeing to be a part of the escape committee. He contributed by copying maps, making clothes from blankets and digging the tunnel. These efforts made it possible for two officers to escape, but they were captured and returned to the camp.

Sherk was in a group of 150 prisoners who were moved on July 15, 1943 to the camp at Rimini on the east coast of Italy. Sherk participated in an escape effort at Rimini as well. Following the capitulation of Italy and the disarray of the Italian forces, the population at the Rimini camp reacted rapidly. The camp was taken over by the prisoners and British officers took command of the group. There was news that the Germans were on their way. The prisoners opened the gates and ran for the high land to make their way to the south. The Germans were on the scene rapidly, and with the use of dogs, they started to recapture the prisoners around Rimini who had not travelled too far.

Sherk and a friend from the camp, an RAF officer named McLarty, were not among the first group who were captured. They were still in the wooded area as the Germans carried out their searches. The men realized that if they moved too fast they could be captured, so they decided to stay in hiding until the main group of searchers had passed their area. As they finally made their move to leave the forest, their luck ran out, and they were quickly captured by a German patrol.

Sherk and McLarty were placed with three others who had also just been captured, and the march back to the camp began. Not long into the journey, the group stopped to rest. Sherk and McLarty quickly convinced their guards to allow them to sit a distance away in the shade. As soon as they were in the shade, the prisoners slipped behind a rock and placed a hat on the rock so that the guards would believe that the two were there. They rushed down a nearby hill to a forest where they found an effective hiding place. The Germans, realizing that the two were gone, carried out a frustrating search. They walked by the hiding place of the two escapees several times before giving up.

Sherk and McLarty learned from their experience and decided to move south carefully, watching for any patrols. As they travelled south, they found two other escapees, one Arab, one Palestinian. The men heard about a cave in a nearby mountain that was a safe haven for escapees because the local people supplied them with food and water.

Thirty escapees were in the area on October 6, 1943, when a German raiding party arrived to capture them. Again, Sherk and McLarty were able to avoid being taken. They were lucky because a local guide showed them the way up the mountain to safety. Soon, they met another two escapees at Campogivde who were waiting for help moving through the front lines to the Allied side.

On October 17, there was a message that the Germans were coming. Sherk and McLarty wasted no time moving toward the front on their own. Shortly after they left, the Germans arrived in the area and shot everyone they saw. They continued in Sherk and McLarty's direction, executing Allied soldiers. The two escapees continued to move south. In six days they arrived in Cupello, Italy, 125 miles south of Rimini. Sherk and McLarty were guided through the front lines on October 25 and arrived at Lucera in the southern Italian province of Foggia. Sherk arrived in London on November 13, 1943.

There are many stories of escapes, but none are alike. The story of Captain Henry "Barney" Byrnes' escape from prison camp P.G. 122, which was just a mile north of Rome, is unique. Byrnes was at the prison camp after he was captured in Sicily on July 24, 1943. When he arrived, only three prisoners were in the camp. A few days later, a British Seaforth major, who had been wandering in the hills with a cast on his leg, joined Byrnes at the camp.

Italy had capitulated and was out of war, and the group of prisoners were to be moved north on September 22 to a German prisoner of war camp. The prisoners were placed on a truck to be taken to the train station. Once the group arrived, they found that the trains were not running. The prisoners were loaded onto the trucks again and taken back to the prison camp. The next day, the group of prisoners marched to another point from which they could be moved north. As they marched, Byrnes' group decided to escape from the Italian guards. When they started to walk across a field away from the guards, one of them lifted his rifle to threaten the Allied soldiers. Byrnes spoke up and told the man to put his rifle down, which he did. The prisoners were planning to make their way around Rome and then travel south to Allied lines. The British Seaforth major and Byrnes travelled together. The rest of the escapees made their own way alone or with partners.

As the major and Byrnes entered the first village, they were met by a friendly local who told them that the Germans were in positions all around the area and the best chance for them was to get to the Vatican and seek sanctuary. The two agreed and started on their way. They expected that once they were in the Vatican, they would stay there until Rome fell to the Allies. The two men were sure that would only take a few days.

As the two walked along, their luck held and a doctor came along the road in a Fiat. The roads were dangerous places because at any moment a German patrol could appear around a corner. They explained their plan to the doctor who agreed to drive them to the Vatican and ask for sanctuary for them. They realized the car was too small for them to sit in with the cast on the Seaforth major's leg. So the major positioned himself with his leg propped out the window.

When the group arrived at the Vatican, they found the Santa Maria Gate opened and unguarded, so the doctor drove in without stopping. Byrnes' luck held as the secretary and the butler to the British ambassador to the Holy See were there. When the guard realized that two prisoners of war were inside the gates and asking for sanctuary, his first reaction was to remove them. Immediately, the two British men insisted that their fellow countryman and Byrnes be given sanctuary.

The reception was cool. The Seaforth major and Byrnes were imprisoned in the gendarme barracks. The Vatican did provide them with good food and wine, and they received parcels with reading material from the British Embassy. As tensions decreased and it was clear that the Allied forces would win the war, the escapees were given more freedom from their prison cells. Soon, they had the privilege of going where they wished in the Vatican. They just had to respect the rules that disallowed them from being in the garden in the afternoon when Pope Pius XII spent time there.

Byrnes had been in the Vatican for nine months when Rome fell to the Allied forces. He was already having regular visits with the British Legation and was working for the Rome escape line. Sir D'Arcy Osborne, British Minister to the Holy See, and his butler, John May, organized the Rome line. The two men had been working to find the names of escaped prisoners of war who were hiding in Rome and the area. Before Rome fell, the Vatican opened its gates, and those in sanctuary were free to come and go as they pleased. The escapees worked to provide support to people in hiding.

The British developed the support system in a cooperative effort with the Swiss government, which was running the Red Cross. Byrnes' work included removing the labels from Red Cross parcels in case the Germans were alerted to where the supplies originated if they were intercepted. The supplies were then carried by runners to escapees and evaders that British officials at the Holy See knew were in hiding. Many people in hiding were in rags and needed clothing. Other people working with the British at the Holy See collected what clothes they could, and runners took these items to the people in hiding too.

The Italians began accepting cheques written to pay for supplies by those active in the Rome escape line. It was clear who was winning the war, so the

Italians believed that the cheques would be good. The cooperation from the local population increased. People started giving the agents of the Rome line a good rate of exchange on the currency, and Italian citizens even gave the escape line members loans. Soon, the effort was receiving funds from the British Foreign Office.

As the organization developed, about 300 escaped prisoners in Rome received support. Another approximately 3000 Allied servicemen were in hiding in the area around Rome. Rural farmers and their families who had no sympathy for the fascists and looked forward to the end of the war assisted many men.

Even before Rome was liberated, plans were underway to establish a network to assist those Italians who had aided escapees and evaders. A large operation was established with key leading people such as British artillery major Sam Derry, who was secretly living in the British Legation in the Vatican before Rome fell.

The operation was to provide for the Italians who had suffered deprivation, the destruction of their homes and the death of their family members at the hands of the Germans. Byrnes was asked to help establish the Allied Control Commission that would determine exactly who had assisted Allied personnel during the war. The Commission was to identify who had helped and what compensation would be provided. Some people were paid money while others received assistance in kind. In one instance, a Roman Catholic order that ran a boys' school had hidden six or seven evaders. The school received football gear including uniforms and balls. All the Italians who had helped evaders received testimonial letters from General Sir Harold Alexander, the main commander of the Allies' land forces during the invasion of Italy.

The Allied Control Commission investigated about 90,000 cases. Sam Derry was promoted and made the commanding officer of the operation. Captain Henry "Barney" Byrnes remained with the operation for about one and half years. By the time he returned to Canada, the war had been over for quite a while.

CHAPTER NINE

Escaping Eastern Camps

DURING WORLD WAR II, THERE WERE MANY PRISONER OF WAR camps in Eastern Germany, Poland and Czechoslovakia (since 1992, the Czech Republic and Slovakia). The prisoners in these remote camps had the same desire to escape that prisoners in other camps had. Many of them were not deterred by their location. For those who did escape, they had advantages that escapees from German prisoner of war camps did not. The men who escaped from prison camps in Germany faced a hostile population. An escapee knew almost certainly that everyone they met during their trek through the country would turn them in, while those in the eastern camps could look for help from the workers and peasants who opposed the occupying Germans. Many people would assist the escaping prisoners with food, clothes, hiding places and information about where they could find safe passage.

Corporal Alex Masterton was at Stalag XX A, near the city of Thorn (or Toru) in Poland early in 1944. He was moved with nine others to a farm prison camp, also in Poland. The entire group was made up of Canadians who had been serving in the British army. After they arrived at the new camp, one of their number died. During the days, prisoners reported to different farms to work. Their guard travelled by bicycle that he rode from one farm to the next. At night, the prisoners and the guard would stay at a small stone farmhouse with some barbed wire around the yard. When the Canadians decided to escape, the process of cutting through the wire was a simple one.

The prisoners knew that there would soon be an Allied landing because they noticed a substantial increase in the number of daytime American bombing runs overhead and they heard the continuous bombing efforts of the British at night. The prisoners talked about the impending invasion and the expected collapse of Germany. They all agreed that the time to escape was coming soon.

The landing occurred, and in late August 1944, five men in Masterton's group decided to escape. They agreed that they should wear their uniforms and make a run south. When they approached the wire fence and cut the wires, they were ready to go, but they waited as a large column of German tanks came down the road in front of the stone farmhouse. After the tanks had passed, the men continued. At dawn, they stepped out across the road on the first leg of their journey to freedom.

To avoid capture, the five men agreed to split up. The group that headed for the nearby forest was quickly captured by a large group of police and soldiers. They were shot on the spot, which was common by that time in the war.

Alex Masterton continued on with two other escapees. They approached a well-kept farm that was obviously owned by a wealthy farmer. Clearly the owner had to be German, so they decided to approach the workers, who were sure to be Poles. Masterton could speak German better than any of the others in his group and agreed to approach the groom, who was working in the barn. The other two hid behind a large manure pile. Masterton stepped forward and introduced himself as an escaped prisoner and asked the Polish man if he would help. The escapees were correct—the worker was a cooperative Pole who agreed to help them. He showed the men where to hide in the barn. Later, he brought them water and food. The three escapees remained in the barn for three days to make sure that the German search was over before they continued on their way.

Before the three left, their Polish host told them that they had to walk back to Thorn as they had to get across the Vistula River by walking over a bridge. The three walked to Thorn. Nearby, they came across a little Polish house, so they knocked at the door and a small man answered. They told him that they were escaped British soldiers and asked if he could help. He agreed right away and told them he was a railroad worker. The Pole told them to meet him at a certain place by the tracks. They agreed and made their way to the spot. Once there, the man put them on a boxcar travelling east. The three escapees were on their way and travelled 94 miles by rail.

It began to rain while the men were on the train. Once the rain stopped, they got off and headed to a nearby large house. They assumed that Germans also owned the house, so they approached the field workers for help. The farm worker they approached was a Pole, and he was willing to help. While the men were hiding, they could hear the gunfire and artillery of the battle on the eastern front. As the hours passed, the battle raged around them. The warfare was followed by a long period of quiet. Then there were voices, and the three men looked out the windows to see Russian soldiers pointing their guns at them. The escapees yelled that they were English prisoners of war.

The Russians searched the three men and took them back to their headquarters east of Thorn. It took three months for Alex Masterton and his two companions to be transferred to Odessa, where they were kept in a compound with the crews of two B-17 bombers that had been shot down while bombing the Ploesti oilfields.

The compound did not have heavy security, and Masterton was able to leave and return. He made his way to the docks and saw a freight ship flying the U.S. flag. The Canadian approached the ship that was delivering supplies for the Russian war effort. A Russian soldier was standing guard, so Alex took out a card that said "Gift of the Canadian Red Cross" and showed it to the soldier, who accepted that it was a pass. Alex boarded the ship and approached a crewman.

Masterton introduced himself as an escaped prisoner of war. He wasted no time asking if he could stay with the ship and travel back to the United States. The crewmember called out to his friends, and they brought out their gramophone. They played Masterton a record of Frank Sinatra. Once they had heard a number of selections, they asked if he was hungry. The sailors took him to a walk-in refrigerator and brought out chicken, ham and oranges. Masterton ate, but he was not used to rich food and vomited over the side of the ship.

The captain was asked if Masterton could stay, and he agreed. The Americans provided a cabin, but a Russian search party arrived with dogs and demanded to search the ship. In a few moments, they found Masterton and he was taken back to the compound.

Two weeks after the Americans left, a British freighter arrived carrying a large crane for the port. The captain of the ship had another mission other than delivering the crane. He had information about the escaped prisoners of war and went to the compound to collect them. The group of escapees was taken to the ship. The news was radioed to the British Counsel in Istanbul. The captain was informed that the men would be accepted there, but they all had to be dressed in civilian clothes because Turkey was neutral.

The group was housed in Istanbul for two weeks while arrangements were made to take them to England. Another British ship came to pick them up. Soon they arrived in Naples, staying there for a week. The group returned to England shortly after Christmas 1944.

CHAPTER TEN

Escaping Stalag Luft III

THE PRISON CAMP NAMED STALAG LUFT III WAS THE SITE OF the most persistent, daring and extraordinary escape efforts of World War II. The Geneva Convention, which outlined the rules of war, stated that it was the duty of each prisoner to try to escape. By the time of the Great Escape, which was one of the last escapes that happened in the war, there had been about 100 tunnels dug by the prisoners. The escapes were not because the conditions at Stalag Luft III were poor, or because the prisoners had been treated badly. In fact, the camp, run by the Luftwaffe, treated prisoners with more respect than other camps. One of the central reasons why these prisoners were exceptional in their efforts to escape was that they were highly motivated, well-trained and disciplined aircrew.

Among the most daring escapes from Stalag Luft III was the Wooden Horse, where the novel idea was to dig a tunnel in the centre of the exercise yard. It was located right in front of the guards who watched the prisoners every day.

The Great Escape, planned and carried out at Stalag Luft III, was the most extraordinary tunnelling effort that had ever been carried out in any prisoner of war camp. The prisoners didn't plan a single tunnel that would take a few prisoners beyond the fences of the camp. The idea was to dig three massive tunnels, named Tom, Dick and Harry, at the same time. The tunnels were masterpieces of deception, with entrances chipped from concrete and trapdoors that opened with hinges. Canadians played central roles in designing the tunnels and carrying out the plans.

The original expectation for the Great Escape was to provide an opportunity for hundreds to escape on a single night and create havoc in Germany. But, like many great plans, it had to take into account difficulties facing the escapees.

Many prisoners saw the process of escaping as an opportunity to tie up as many resources of the Germans as possible in searching for and recapturing them. The search and recapture effort would take men away from the front lines. Hitler was worried about Allied soldiers escaping. A massive foreign work force in Germany was necessary to the Nazi war machine. Many of these workers were forced labour, and it was feared that escaped Allied officers could become leaders of the workers. The result could be a fifth column of enemy within Germany's borders.

All of the prisoners who entered the tunnel to escape when the day came expected that they would simply be recaptured and returned to the camp, the normal policy in such cases. None of the escapees or officers who ran Stalag Luft III imagined the rage of Hitler when he heard about the mass escapes. Hitler was so angered by the magnitude of the escapes that he ordered the murder of 50 of the escapees. None of the escapees could have calculated that he would order the systematic murder of soldiers, contrary to the Geneva Convention.

Allied aircrews bombed Europe throughout World War II. German cities and towns like Berlin, Dresden, Hamburg, Augsburg, Braunschweig, Kassel, Pforzheim and Würzburg were bombed by the Allied forces. Other targets included dams like the Möhne Dam, Eder Dam, Sorpe Dam, Lister Dam, Sorpe Dam and Ennepe Dam. Many aircrews found themselves behind enemy lines because they were shot down or made forced landings.

The Germans wanted to create a simplified system to administer and handle the prisoners of war. To do so, they built camps that were run by each of their services, including the navy, air force (Luftwaffe) and army. The German word for a prison was *Stalag*. In the case of the prisoner of war camp Stalag Luft III, the name referred to a prison camp that was run by the Luftwaffe. *Stalag Luft* was a shortened form of *Stammlager Luft*, meaning permanent camp.

The Luftwaffe was made up of more educated members than the other German military services. The members of the Luftwaffe displayed the least support for the Nazi doctrine in Germany. They generally had more respect for Allied aircrew than other German forces such as the army or the SS.

The prison camp, Stalag Luft III, was near Sagan, Germany, which later became Zagan in Poland. The Luftwaffe prison camps generally followed the Geneva Convention, but the prisoners, like the guards, faced the ongoing problem of insufficient food rations. Many of the prisoners were able to improve their situations with the regular arrivals of Red Cross parcels as well as parcels sent by family members and various charities.

Clothing, like food, was a problem in the prison camps. Civilian clothing was forbidden because it would allow men to escape and blend into the population. The result was that new clothing would include army-issued uniforms or clothing made to appear as a military uniform. The badges and crests from the airmen's uniforms were carefully attached to whatever clothes were available. When a prisoner found a piece of civilian clothing, it was hidden. All the prisoners who escaped and hoped to be successful had to have a set of civilian clothes. At the same time, those who wore civilian clothes during an escape had to carry their badges and tags from their uniforms. If they were captured, they had to show the pieces of their uniforms to demonstrate they weren't spies.

The Geneva Convention also set out rules for the conduct of prisoners in camps during war. It was accepted that those who were in prison should continue to wear their uniforms and salute their enemy captors as they would their own officers. Within prisoner of war camps, standard military discipline continued, whether a soldier was a German or an Allied soldier.

The escapes that did occur at Stalag Luft III were made possible by the sheer size of the camp. As the war progressed, repeated expansions meant that the camp grew to 10,000 prisoners. It covered an area of 59 acres, and five miles of fence surrounded it. With such a large population and so much area for the guards to patrol, there were many opportunities for escapees to exploit. With such a large population at Stalag Luft III, there was a good array of men with expertise in escape as well as talent in forging, tailoring clothes and tunnelling.

The Wooden Horse Escape, which occurred at Stalag Luft III, was one of the most famous escapes during World War II. One participant, Flight Lieutenant Dallas Laskey, had just arrived at Luft III when he developed a swelling on the back of his head. He went to the prison camp hospital to have it treated. In the hospital, he met a fellow prisoner, Eric Williams, who told him about the Wooden Horse plan and asked if he wanted to help. Dallas immediately agreed.

The Wooden Horse Escape got its name from the use of a vaulting horse used in gymnastics. It was a box with a padded top and a wide bottom that was about seven feet long. The vaulting horse had a pyramid shape. The prisoners took it out each day and placed it in exactly the same spot each time so that the prisoners could use it in the prison ground for exercise.

Inside the horse, a man was digging a tunnel. Under the vaulting horse, a trap door was covered in sand. The digger would start each day by digging the sand from the top of the trap door. He would open the trap door, climb in and then start digging the tunnel. The dirt from the digging process was loaded into prepared boxes inside the vaulting horse. At the end of each day, the gymnasts had to pick up the vaulting horse with the sand, dirt and digger inside. They strained to carry it back each day in front of the Germans so that the guards did not notice that the vaulting horse was far too heavy.

Flight Lieutenant Dallas Laskey had experience in university gymnastics and played the role of coach. There had to be a lot of activity going on to keep the vaulting horse in place throughout the day, so many clumsy men had their turn vaulting over the horse. One Englishman was so clumsy that he was given the nickname "Harry the Horse." One day he hit the horse instead of going over it, and the vaulting horse fell over, exposing the digging operation. The men quickly gathered around, keeping the German guards from seeing what was going on. The vaulting horse was pulled back up into position. On another day, "Harry the Horse" made it over the vaulting horse, but he landed with such intensity on the other side that the tunnel underneath caved in. Laskey fell down over the caved-in tunnel and pretended to have hurt himself. The other men quickly gathered around and covered up the hole.

To speed up the progress, the escape committee agreed to have three diggers work on the tunnel. To get the three men into the tunnel, the men staged adjustments to the vaulting horse to get the extra men in and out during each day of digging. The tunnel diggers were Ollie Philpot, Michael Codner and Eric Williams.

Once the tunnel was complete, Philpot, Codner and Williams escaped. They made their way to the train station, bought tickets and made it out of Germany on a ship to Sweden.

The escape committee decided that the second group to leave should include Dallas Laskey along with men called Rawley and Lubbock. But before they could leave, the tunnel was discovered by Germans at about 9:30 PM. Laskey admitted later that he was not too upset by losing his chance to escape because he had the difficult task of escaping to the east. He was to go through Czechoslovakia and south to Yugoslavia to assist the guerrillas fighting the Germans in the region.

The response from the Germans when they discovered the tunnel was to rush into the prison barracks to take a roll call to find out how many had escaped and who they were. The commandant, guards and soldiers were screaming as men came and left the barracks and others fused the lights. The Germans gave up their head count after it became clear that they would not make any headway.

The prisoners answered a roll call early the next morning. A table was set up, and there were photographs of the prisoners in boxes before the guards to make sure they had exactly whom they called. The prisoners again refused to cooperate. One of them found a soccer ball and started to kick it from one side of the prison compound to the other. A large group of prisoners started to chase the ball and did not respond when their names were called.

There was no effective roll call by lunch, and so the prisoners left for lunch. A bugle call for another roll call came after lunch. As the prisoners came out of their barracks, they found that a large contingent of armed German soldiers had taken positions near the gate. Members of the Gestapo were with the group of soldiers. The prisoners quickly formed the required lines, and a full roll call was completed.

The German reaction was swift—the water and electricity were cut off to the prisoners. The guards told the prisoners that the wheel on the wagon was broken, which meant that the Red Cross parcels would not arrive. The prisoners faced about six months with half their usual rations. There were no privileges either, which included walks and visits to nearby camps. The prisoners had to march in five parades a day, and no window could be opened at night, regardless of how hot it was.

Many prisoners enjoyed the golf course at the camp. The Germans believed that the prisoners had carried the sand from the tunnels and poured it into the bunkers on the course. But the sand had not been poured into the sand traps at the golf course. The subsurface sand was a bright yellow, and when the guards saw it on the ground they would search for a tunnel. Prisoners who had long narrow bags strapped to their legs had to carefully mix the sand from the Wooden Horse tunnel with sand from the surface. They would walk around the camp releasing a little at a time. Sometimes a prisoner was not careful enough and released too much sand at once. A long streak of bright yellow sand appeared on the ground and had to be quickly kicked to blend with the surface sand.

Many prisoners who worked hard on the tunnel and then remained in the prison camp later suffered the consequences, but they said that being in the camp was made more bearable by knowing that the escapees had made it to Sweden.

The most famous, complex and tragic World War II escape was the Great Escape at Stalag Luft III. The prisoners of war at the camp developed a complex escape plan that saw the construction of three tunnels named Tom, Dick and Harry. The Harry tunnel provided an escape route for 76 Allied officers to travel 350 feet underground to the outside of the fences of the camp. Only three made it to freedom. The escape brought the strongest reaction ever from the Gestapo—50 of those captured were executed. The original plan was for hundreds of prisoners to escape.

As the Stalag Luft III grew in size to about 10,000 prisoners, the best and most experienced potential escapees were brought together. The men intent on escaping easily found the best forgers, tailors, tunnel builders and security men.

The leading organizers of the Great Escape included Squadron Leader Roger J. Bushell, who was the commanding officer of No. 922 Squadron. In May 1940, his Spitfire was shot down as he participated in the Battle of France. Bushell escaped and found a hiding place in Prague, but he was captured following the Heydrich assassination.

Reinhard Heydrich was second in command in Germany after Adolf Hitler. Heydrich was the chief of the Reich Main Security Office, which had control over the Gestapo, the Security Agency and the Criminal Police. In this role, Heydrich systematically found and killed Hitler's enemies in Germany. Hitler credited him with providing the personal security he needed to be the dictator of Germany. Heydrich was also credited with coming up with the "Final Solution," which was what the Nazis called the genocide of the Jewish people. After the Germans gave Heydrich the title of "Protector of Bohemia and Moravia," the Special Operations Executive (SOE) carried out a successful plan to assassinate him in Prague on May 27, 1942. The Nazis' response was widespread killings of Czech citizens in retribution.

During his capture, Bushell witnessed the Gestapo's execution of the family who hid him. The experience left Bushell with an intense hatred for the Germans, which his better treatment at Stalag Luft III did not change.

The leader for the escape committee was Group Captain Harry "Wings" Day who had been with No. 57 Squadron when he was shot down on October 13, 1939. From 1939 until 1942, Day was imprisoned at Stalag Luft III. In October 1942, Day was transferred to the Offizierlager XXIB, an officers' camp. Group Commander Herbert M. Massey, who had been a World War I fighter pilot, replaced him at Luft III.

Bushell was the leader of the escape committee executive that organized the Great Escape. Those directly involved included Flying Officer Wally Floody, Peter "Hornblower" Fanshawe and Flight Lieutenant George R. Harsh from No. 102 Squadron.

Bushell began the work that started the Great Escape by first identifying and recruiting the best forgers, tailors, tunnel diggers and surveillance men. In the meetings with those selected, Bushell announced that he was developing an operation that would allow 250 prisoners to escape. The plan included a group of well-prepared escapees equipped with all the clothing, forged documents and maps needed to make their way back to the Allied side. There would also be a large number of other escapees who might be able to return to England, but if not, their main purpose was to create a large a problem as possible for the Germans. This second group of escapees would have a minimum of forged documents or none at all. They could wear whatever they wanted while escaping. These escapees were called "hard-arsers," and they would try to get as far as they could before they were captured.

Roger Bushell pursued his escape plan with great intensity even though the German authorities had warned him that any further escape attempts by him would result in execution.

Canadian Flight Officer Wally Floody played a central role in the Great Escape—he was a mining engineer at Kirkland Lake, Ontario, before the war and accepted the responsibility to dig the tunnels. Although Floody had experience in mining hard rock, his knowledge of using explosives to mine hard rock was meaningless—the escape tunnels had to be dug by hand through soft sand.

Floody was able to complete the tunnel by using good common sense in the job. Flight Lieutenant R.G. "Crump" Ker-Ramsey, Henry "Johnny" Marshall and many others helped Floody.

The group needed as many escape kits as possible. These kits included maps and compasses that were designed by Johnny Travis and a team he organized. They used broken parts of Bakelite gramophone records that were melted down and formed into the needed shapes. The men made the needles for the compasses from cut slivers of razor blades that they magnetized.

Flight Lieutenant Des Plunkett headed a team of men who copied maps for the escape kits. Other escape team members stole necessary identification papers or bribed prison staff to obtain them. They gave the original papers to a team led by Flight Lieutenant "Tim" Walenn, who produced forgeries. These two groups earned the nickname "Dean and Dawson," which was a reference to a well-known travel agency.

Once the escapees made it out of the prison, they had to either hide, if they were in uniform, or blend into the population with clothes that appeared to be civilian. A group headed by Tommy Guest handled the production of civilian clothes. They took uniforms and cut and refit them to appear to be worker clothes.

Once the various items for the escapees were finished, they were hidden in compartments in the prisoners' barracks. Pilot Officer "Digger" Macintosh and his team of carpenters created hiding places for these items.

There was a constant need for documents, such as maps and train schedules, that appeared to be authentic. The escape committee members were often astonished at the number of prison guards who cooperated with them. The guards provided everything needed for the operation, so the forgers had detailed documents and a clear idea of what was needed to travel in Germany.

The German guards even provided detailed information about the landscape around Stalag Luft III. These details included where the train stations were and how they were laid out so that escapees could quickly find the station, get their tickets and board the train. For detailed information and documents, the prisoners bribed the guards with items such as cigarettes, chocolate or soap that were available from the Red Cross parcels.

In several cases, when a guard appeared to be less intelligent, those prisoners bribing him would write out the transaction and have the guard sign it. The guard was told that the receipt was needed to account for the missing items that he had received. The guard would then be blackmailed with the threat that the signed note would be presented to the camp commandant. The blackmail proved effective in obtaining a camera and film. Equipment to develop the film followed.

Forging documents was a painstaking endeavour. Each paper needed to have every detail in place, including photographs. The documents were marked with many different rubber stamps, which changed often during the war, making it difficult to get them right. These stamps had to be applied with different ink colours, and they had to be detailed.

The documents needed to travel as a worker were substantial. They included a document called a *Dienstausweise* that gave the holder permission to be on the property of the German defence force. A military leave pass called a *Ruckkehrscheine* was issued to foreign workers so that they could return home. The escapees needed a identity card, the *Kennkarte*. Those travelling also needed a visa called a *Sichtvermark*. Other documents included a pass, called an *Ausweise,* and a temporary pass, *Vorlaufweise*. These detailed documents would take the forgers weeks to complete.

The prisoners had nicknames for the various Germans that they had contact with. The guards were universally called "goons." The towers around the perimeter of the camp, manned by German guards, were called "goon towers." These towers had searchlights and machine guns. The men who were in these towers were known to be less professional than other guards. Many guards were at the prison camps after being removed from full military duties. The men in the goon towers were known for being trigger-happy. Prisoners who passed beyond the knee-high warning wire and did not heed the guards' calls were often shot. Written complaints by the prisoners to the commandant described the excessive use of firearms by the guards in the towers.

As cases of prisoners tunnelling to escape the camps continued elsewhere, the Germans developed specialists in finding evidence of tunnels in prison camps. These men were called "ferrets." When the ferrets arrived, they could go wherever they wanted and enter any building that they wanted without warning. They arrived with metal probes that they would push into the ground to find a tunnel below. They searched for the brighter yellow sand on the ground as well, which indicated that sand from below the surface was being disposed of in the prison's yard. Some ferrets spoke English, and they would crawl under barracks and listen to the men's conversation to find out what was going on. When the ferrets or the guards did detect tunnelling, they would not act immediately. They would watch the work progress, and then as the tunnel progressed to completion, heavy trucks or equipment would be brought in to drive over the tunnels and collapse them.

To defeat the ferrets, a comprehensive security operation was put into place at Stalag Luft III. Flight Lieutenant George Harsh, who was an American airman serving with the RCAF, headed the security operation. He was with No. 102 Squadron when he was shot down on the night of October 5, 1942. Harsh set up a rotation of officers who tracked every movement of every guard and ferret in the camp. This operation was called the "Duty Pilot" system. The system included a series of signals that relayed to everyone in the camp who was around and where they were. The effect of this system was that every member of the escape effort could cover up what he was doing if a guard or ferret came too close. Often, prisoners were able to appear like they were pursuing hobbies. A watch was always out for Corporal Gefreiter Greise, who was among the most effective ferrets. He was nicknamed "Rubberneck."

The Germans made several attempts to stop the system of prisoner surveillance, but they finally gave up. At one time, the Germans asked the members of the Duty Pilot system to testify when one of the German guards had not fulfilled his duties and left work early.

The plan to escape Stalag Luft III was created with an understanding of the obstacles the escapees would face from the Germans. The plan called for three tunnels, named Tom, Dick and Harry, with the expectation that the ferrets or guards would find one of two of them. The prisoners concealed the tunnelling so that if the ferrets crawled under the barracks where there was a space, they would never find the opening as they had in other escape attempts. There were brick and concrete platforms in each barrack hut where the stoves were placed. The Tom tunnel was dug in Hut 105 and passed through the concrete and brick platform under the stoves. This was also how the entrance of the Harry tunnel was created in Hut 104. The tunnel engineers carefully chipped the concrete pad under the stoves so that it could be lifted when the stove was moved to one side. When the concrete lid was lifted for the first time, it was placed on hinges so that it could be rapidly opened to allow the diggers and later the escapees to enter the tunnels. This system of trap doors worked well. In one instance, the men replaced a trap door and moved a stove back into place with only 20 seconds of warning.

The Dick tunnel was concealed under a drainpipe in the shower room in Hut 122. This entrance was sealed well and could be covered effectively under a couple feet of water when the ferrets were around. The result was that the Germans never discovered Dick.

Dispersing the sand from the three massive operations to build Tom, Dick and Harry became one of the most onerous and serious problems for the escape plan. All it would take was a momentary lapse and the guards could see the bright yellow sand. The sand was loaded into long, narrow bags that were placed inside the prisoners' pants and then released as they walked around the grounds. These workers were called "Penguins."

The tunnelling process was dangerous with hazards both above and below the ground. A risk of cave-ins always existed for the diggers working on the front face of the tunnel. Cave-ins often happened with no warning at all. The sand would rush in around the man, and it was up to the second helper at the front of the tunnel to quickly dig out the victim. No one died, but some men who experienced the suffocation had to take days off to recover.

Collapsed tunnels presented some immediate problems. A collapsed tunnel would create a large dome of sand that had to be moved so that reinforcements could be built up. Then sand had to be packed up above the section again.

The tunnels were reinforced with about 4000 bed boards. These boards were removed from the prisoners' beds. The prisoners adapted to sleeping on beds that had few boards to support them. As the tunnelling went on, the bed frames supported hammocks made of string—all the boards were finally removed from the beds for use in the tunnels. The size of the bedboards dictated the size of the tunnels. The average size was about two feet by two feet.

The operation did have additional hazards, such as what happened to "Cookie" Long. He received a concussion when he was at the bottom of the hole leading to a tunnel, which was 30 feet below the entrance. A bed board fell down and hit him on the head. Another prisoner also suffered head injuries when a German water container that was being used to haul sand out of the tunnel fell down and hit him on the head.

With such long tunnels, the men needed to pump air to those working at the face. Large chambers were dug out at the base of the entrances to house air pumps and handle the sand as it was being sent down the line for dispersal. The air was transported to the front of the tunnels through empty powdered milk tins or other tins that were placed under the floor of the tunnel and sealed with waxed string or tape. The air intake was rigged into the chimney of the stove above.

As work progressed and the tunnels became rather long, the volume of the sand from the front of the digging became too much for individuals to carry. To carry the sand effectively, a small wooden rail car was built. The rail car was set on a wood track made to accommodate these wooden cars.

The long tunnels were dark and difficult to work in. The escape committee wanted to find a way to light them. Joe "Red" Nobel, a RCAF pilot, found a coil of 800 feet of electrical cable that was abandoned by a German workman at the camp and stole it for lighting in the tunnels. The German workman did not report that the wire had gone missing. After the Great Escape, the Gestapo identified the worker and executed him for the oversight.

As the tunnels progressed and the plans were carried out, the Germans had a clear idea that an escape was being prepared. Ferrets worked hard to find the tunnels, but the precautions of the escape committee and the depth of the tunnels saved them from discovery. Then the Germans changed their approach. They developed a list of 19 of the most likely men to be involved in the plan and moved them without notice to Stalag VIIIC, which was at Belaria. Six of the key organizers were moved at this time, but the escape plan was so well established that the second-in-command of each section took over the work. The investigation missed Bushell, and he continued as a senior leader of the escape committee.

In another effort to reduce the risk of a major escape, all the American prisoners were moved to a separate compound. This effort also failed to slow the pace of work on the tunnels. The guards had placed strict controls on communication between the British and the American prisoners, but a semaphore expert sent messages from a hut where the guards could not see him.

The Dick tunnel had to be abandoned because the place where it was to surface outside the fence was cleared to make way for another expansion of the prison camp. However, the abandoned tunnel provided a new place for all those working on forged documents and clothes to work and store their materials. It also became the new dumping place for the sand removed from the other tunnels.

Eventually, so much sand was being dug from the other tunnels that Dick was filled. The escape committee had to find another place to move the sand from the digging. The searchers found that there was a large empty space under the seats of the camp's theatre and decided to create a hole under one of the seats to dump the sand in. Seat number 13 was placed on well-camouflaged hinges.

The escape committee's worst fears were realized in the summer of 1943 when a ferret found the entrance of the nearly complete Tom tunnel. Prisoners had mixed feelings as the Germans destroyed the tunnel. Many of the men regretted the work that had been lost. Yet the men knew it was because of this possibility that they had planned and dug three tunnels. All their efforts turned to the completion of the Harry tunnel.

Harry was completed in March 1944 and measured 336 feet from the bottom of the entrance hole to the exit. If the 28-foot shaft down to the beginning of the horizontal tunnel was included, the tunnel measured over 360 feet long.

The escape committee set priorities for the order in which the escapees would leave through the tunnel. The prisoners who would leave first had the best chances of making it back to England. These men had previous experience in escaping, could speak German and had contributed the most to the escape effort. These escapees were provided with the best documentation, civilian clothes and German currency. They were disguised as foreign workers who could not speak German. Adding to the possibility of success for the escapees was that foreign workers often had papers that were out of order and had some documents missing.

The majority of those following this select group were called "hard-arsers." These low-priority escapees wore whatever they wanted to. They were provided with nearly no documentation. Their plan was to hide and sleep during the days and walk long distances by night. They had few rations, and with the winter conditions in Germany in March, many of them would be up against bad odds. They knew that their chances of success were low, but their main purpose was to create as much confusion as possible and drain as many resources as they could from the German military and security forces.

With the discovery of the Tom tunnel and the ongoing efforts of the German ferrets, the men urgently wanted to get the escape underway as soon as the tunnel Harry was competed. A number of problems occurred on the night of the escape on March 24. The weather was too cold because the temperatures were dropping to below freezing at night. The hard-arsers would have had better success if the temperature had been warmer. In such conditions, the forests were wet and cold with few good hiding places.

The prisoners who were to escape made their way to Hut 104 as darkness fell. They had to be in place before the curfew in the camp. Anyone out of the huts after dark would be shot. Some of the men were nearly overcome with nervousness as they watched a German soldier walk into the hut unannounced. They stared in a moment of disbelief when they realized that Flight Officer Pawel Tobolski was disguised as a German soldier for his escape.

Another problem facing the escapees was that the tunnel surfaced about 30 yards short of the desired exit location, a wooded area beyond the fence. Johnny Bull discovered the shortfall at 10:15 PM. The first escapee was on his way at 10:30 PM. Added to this difficulty, the entrance was only 30 feet from the closest watchtower. To the relief of the escapees, the guards in the watchtowers concentrated on the compound below and not the area outside the fence, but there were regular patrols of Germans who walked with their dogs between the forested area and the fence.

The escapees waited for a signal to make their way out of the tunnel and make a dash for the forest. The men left tracks from the end of the tunnel to the forest because of the fresh snow. Trying to avoid the gaze of the watchtower and patrols slowed the escapees considerably.

The escape was already going badly as there was poor communication between those coordinating the escapees leaving the tunnel and those marshalling the men into the passageway. Getting the men through the tunnel was already going slowly when the lights went out because an air raid made the Germans cut all power to the camp. The men had to use fat lamps to light their way.

A message was finally sent back to send a long rope that would be used to signal when the men could come and when they would have to wait for a patrolling German to pass by. Clearly there was a problem at the entrance, but no one could find out what it was. The escapees were apprehensive as the flow of men through the tunnel was reduced to about 12 men every hour. The expectation was that there would be about one man out every minute. Finally, the men at the front sent a message back to let everyone know that they would not be able to move more than 100 men out. The prisoners who had numbers higher than 100 lay down on the floor of the hut and waited for daylight. By the end of the process, only 76 made it out.

The escape continued until 4:55 AM. From the forest, Flight Lieutenant Langlois, who had been with No. 12 Squadron when he was shot down on August 5, 1941, was watching the German patroller change from his regular path. His new route would take him within a few feet of the entrance of the tunnel exit. Flight Lieutenant Shand was ready to exit the tunnel and run for the trees beyond. Langlois had been using a single jerk on the rope to tell the escapees to wait, and he did the same thing at that moment. Shand thought it was a signal to move on quickly and emerged from the tunnel. At that moment he was right near the feet of the guard. The guard was just passing the tunnel and still did not see the steam rising from those inside waiting for the chance to move up. The German did not notice the well-marked tracks in the fresh snow for several moments. He slowly watched the motion of Langlois before he suddenly realized that something was not right. He lifted his rifle and quickly fired a shot in Langlois' direction, but he missed by a wide margin. The guard grabbed his whistle and blew repeatedly and loudly. The escaped prisoners in the woods, including Langlois, ran as fast as they could. The guard apprehended Squadron Leader McBride, who waiting at the exit of the tunnel. Len Trent, who was at the edge of the woods, surrendered.

The men in the tunnel panicked, believing that a ferret would jump down the entrance of the tunnel and start shooting. Ken "Shag" Rees and Clive Saxelby were to be the next ones out after McBride, and they rushed back up the tunnel as soon as they heard the shots. Rees was the last man returning up the tunnel, so he tried to take out the support at the end of the tunnel and collapse the roof. The support was too well built, and he could not rip down the roof by kicking at it, so he followed Saxelby out.

The men who had been in the tunnel hurriedly gathered in hut 104. The men worked quickly to burn their identification papers. They ate the rations they had packed for the journey because they were sure the Germans would take them away as soon as they were discovered.

Once the German ferrets arrived with their dogs, they still could not find the entrance to the tunnel. The dogs found a comfortable pile of coats and fell asleep. The Germans decided that the only way to find the entrance was to go out to the exit and crawl up the tunnel. They sent the ferret Charlie Pilz, and Pilz still could not find the entrance as he stood under it yelling for help. The Allied servicemen listened for a while. Then they felt sorry for the ferret and finally let him out. Charlie Pilz climbed out of the tunnel and told the men in the hut that he thought it was the best tunnel he had ever seen.

The escapees continued to face difficulties. A large group of them arrived at the train station, but they had a hard time finding the entrance in the dark. The problem was that the entrance was situated right under the platform through a narrow enclosure. Once the men found their way into the train station, they had missed their train and had to wait for the next. They milled around waiting and acting as though they did not know each other.

The escapees who waited until daylight caught the train. A number of them decided not to wait and started walking. Nearly all of these men were apprehended around Sagan before they could leave the region.

News of the large escape made its way to the highest level. Hitler demanded that every escapee be shot. A national alert directed German troops, the police, the Gestapo and the Home Guard to search, find and apprehend the escapees. Hitler's order was against the Geneva Convention and was unthinkable to many. Other German leaders such as Hermann Wilhelm Göring, Feldmarschall Wilhelm Keitel, Major General Von Graevenitz and Major General Adolf Westhoff tried to convince Hitler to rescind the order. Hitler decided that over half of the escapees should be shot and that they were to be cremated. These orders were sent to the Gestapo headquarters, where Dr. Hans Merton and General Artur Nebe wrote an execution list of 50 escapees.

When prisoners of war were recaptured after an escape, the usual practice was to transfer them to the civilian police. This time the order was to send them to the Gestapo. As soon as the recaptured prisoners were handed over to the Gestapo, the Allied servicemen were taken into the country. While they relieved themselves, they were shot. The Gestapo members then returned to their offices to fill out reports that stated that the prisoners had asked to relieve themselves but instead had attempted to escape, so the Germans had responded by shooting them.

Out of the 76 escapees, 73 were recaptured, and the Gestapo murdered 50 of them. Six of the murdered escapees were Canadians. Seventeen men were taken back to Sagan and Stalag Luft III. Four of the recaptured men were sent to the Oflag IX A/H prisoner of war camp near Spangenberg. Two of the escapees were sent to the formidable Colditz Castle, from which few ever escaped.

By the middle of July 1944, the story of the atrocities reached England and British Foreign Minister Anthony Eden, who declared in the British House of Commons that those who carried out the crime would be prosecuted.

The German authorities arrived shortly after the Great Escape at Stalag Luft III, and the commandant, Lindeiner-Wildau, was arrested because he was held responsible for the escape. He faced a trial and was sentenced to a fortress arrest for two years. He served his sentence and was released.

The new commandant, Oberst Braune, took over Stalag Luft III. Braune called Group Captain Herbert M. Massey, the senior British officer, for a meeting. In prisoner of war camps, the Geneva

Convention sets out rules of conduct that state that those imprisoned are not criminals and that the prisoners remain military personnel. Rank continues to be recognized regardless of what uniform one is wearing. So the Allied prisoners had to salute a German soldier with a superior rank. In the same way, German officers and British officers had to treat each other with professionalism and familiarity. This was not the case when Massey met Braune. There was no handshake at the beginning of the meeting, and Braune did not address Massey directly. Braune spoke to Massey through his interpreter, Squadron Leader "Wank" Murray.

Braune told Massey that as of April 6, 1944, the Gestapo had shot and killed 41 of the escapees as they attempted to escape. Their remains would be brought to him as soon as possible. Massey was shocked by the news and asked how many had been wounded. The reply that none had been wounded made it clear that they had been murdered. Braune finished by telling Massey that he could not tell him any more about what had happened.

When Massey shared the information with the prisoners, they were horrified. They realized that they would be shot if they attempted to escape. Hauptmann Pieber, the adjutant of the Luftwaffe, told Massey later that the Luftwaffe had nothing to do with the killings. Days later, a list of the murdered men was given to Massey, and it contained 47 names. This list was updated again to bring the number of murders to 50.

Because of the opposition the Luftwaffe had to the murders, the prisoners at Stalag Luft III were allowed to build a memorial to the victims. Squadron Leader John Hartnell-Beavis designed the memorial. Hartnell-Beavis had been with No. 10 Squadron when he was shot down during the night of July 25, 1943, in a Halifax II. The squadron leader was an architect before he entered the service during World War II.

The urns containing the ashes of the 50 murdered escapees were buried in the cemetery at the prison. After the war, the memorial and the urns were transferred to the Old Garrison Cemetery at Poznan, where they remain today.

* * *

Today, trees grow over most of the area where Stalag Luft III was located. There is little to mark the camp, but a shallow depression runs across the landscape exactly where the Harry tunnel ran. The only museum is tiny. A local man gathered artifacts from the prison.

After the Allies' victory there was a keen interest in finding the Gestapo who murdered the 50 escapees from Stalag Luft III. Those who investigated the murders included Wing Commander Wilfred "Freddie" Bowes, Flight Lieutenant Francis McKenna,

Flight Lieutenant "Dickie" Lyon, Flight Lieutenant Stephen Courtney, Flight Lieutenant Harold Harrison and Wing Officer H.J. Williams, a member of the Royal Air Force Special Investigation Branch. These men systematically travelled across Europe to find those who had murdered the escapees. Once the murderers were identified, they were brought to the London Cage, where an Army Intelligence officer, Lieutenant Colonel A.P. Scotland, questioned them.

Among those who were brought to the London Cage was General Walter Grosch, the senior Luftwaffe officer who had responsibility for the welfare of prisoners in Germany during the war. General Grosch who, like other senior officers of the Luftwaffe, was outraged by the murders, cooperated fully with Scotland Yard and provided critical information. Another key witness was Peter Mohr, a civilian who was employed by the *Kriminalpolizei*. Horrified by what he had seen and heard, Mohr directed the investigators to those responsible.

Those suspects who were found and questioned were brought before a court that was presided over by Court President Major General H.L. Longden. Mr. C.L. Stirling was the Judge Advocate. A six-member panel made up of senior officers included two RAF Wing Commanders, three Army Colonels and a RAF Air Commodore. The court had 10 German lawyers who made up the defence for the accused. The court pronounced 13 of the accused guilty of murder on September 3, 1947. They were hanged for their crimes early in February 1948 at Hamelin Gaol in Hamburg.

CHAPTER ELEVEN

Those Who Made It Home

A CLEAR DIFFERENCE EXISTED BETWEEN THE EXPERIENCES OF men who escaped from either prisoner of war camps or from occupied countries during World War I and World War II.

Those who made their way back to England during World War I were considered potential spies. They were given routine work or were sent back to their home countries.

Those who successfully escaped during World War II were respected for their efforts. In fact, attempting to escape was considered a duty. Once an escapee found himself in one of the occupied countries, Resistance organizations assisted him on his way. In London, Military Intelligence 9 (MI9) specifically trained and sent agents into occupied countries to assist those who were escaping or evading the Germans. They also set up support systems with agents in North Africa and Asia as well. The networks of local Resistance workers and agents became so effective during the war that about 50 percent of all aircrew who went down in occupied countries made it back to England.

Once the war was over, the escapees were like other servicemen and wanted to enjoy comfortable civilian lives. Like other veterans, they wanted to live in security and prosperity.

Peter Anderson arrived in London on October 2, 1915, to face suspicions about whether he was a German spy. Escapes were rare during World War I (see chapter 1, for Anderson's escape story). The authorities who were assessing Anderson thought that an escaped 47-year-old man with a German accent was likely a spy. They never considered that it was his age and his ability to speak German that made his escape a success. They also were unsophisticated in assessing what to look for in spies. The suspicions that the British and the Canadians had of Anderson demonstrated how little they knew about spying at the time. As well, the authorities had a full record of who he was and his military service, which made their suspicions more incredible. After being unable to prove that he was a spy, the authorities decided to place Anderson in Shorncliffe as a staff member and trainer for new recruits. In such a position, they reasoned, he would not be able to report any vital information to the enemy about what was happening at the front.

Anderson's family was living in Edmonton, Alberta, and the news of his escape did not slow their efforts to take ownership of his successful brickworks in the city.

Peter Anderson returned to active duty at Murmansk in the fighting against the Bolsheviks from 1918 to 1919. He received a Distinguished Service Order (DSO) for gallantry in the fight. After he received this award, he finally received a DSO for being the only Canadian officer to escape during World War I.

The prisoners who escaped during the world wars often wanted to continue their contribution to the war effort. During World War I, there was too much paranoia and a lack of understanding about what motivated escapees. Many of those who did successfully escape were treated with suspicion, and they were given non-combat duties or were sent home. Some, like Canadian Peter Anderson, did have opportunities to serve and received the recognition they deserved for their courage and bravery.

During World War II, many escapees who had been taken in by the Resistance in the occupied countries were not sent back to the front or did not return to flying over enemy territory—they had information about the Resistance that the Allies could not afford to lose to the Germans or Axis allies. These men were sent to other duties or sent home. Others, like Lucien Dumais, proved their ability to operate in occupied France and were recruited by MI9 to assist others in escaping. The Canadian team of Dumais and Raymond Labrosse (see chapter 5) worked in occupied France to establish the Shelburne escape network that brought 307 Allied servicemen, including airmen and agents, out of France. The Shelburne operation brought hundreds of escapees right to the heavily German-guarded Brittany coast to be picked up and taken back across the English Channel.

Once the war ended, those who escaped and made it back to Canada focused on living a life of security and prosperity. They took jobs, and many had families, while others suffered the effects of being prisoners of war. Their courage and determination was aimed in a new direction: building Canada into the prosperous world leader it has become today.

Notes on Sources

Bishop, William Arthur. *Unsung Courage: 20 Stories of Canadian Valour and Sacrifice 1939–1945.* Toronto: HarperCollins Publishers, 2001.

Canada. Veterans Affairs Canada. *Uncommon Courage: Canadian Secret Agents in the Second World War.* Ottawa: Public Affairs Division, Veteran Affairs Canada, 1985.

Cassidy, G. L. *Warpath: The Story of the Algonquin Regiment, 1939–1945.* Toronto: Ryerson Press, 1948.

Dancocks, Daniel George. *In Enemy Hands: Canadian Prisoners of War, 1939–45.* Edmonton: Hurtig Publishers, 1983.

Dear, Ian. *Escape and Evasion: POW Breakouts in World War II.* London: Rigel Publications, 2004.

Foot, M. R. D., and Langley, J. M. *MI9: The British Secret Service That Fostered Escape and Evasion, 1939–1945, and Its American Counterpart.* Toronto: The Bodley Head, 1979.

MacLaren, Roy. *Canadians Behind Enemy Lines, 1939–1945.* Vancouver: UBC Press, 2004.

McClung, Nellie L. *Three Times and Out Told by Private Simmons.* Toronto: Thomas Allen, 1918.

Millar, George Reid. *Road to Resistance: An Autobiography.* Toronto: The Bodley Head, 1979.

Morton, Desmond. *Silent Battle: Canadian Prisoners of War in Germany, 1914–1919*. Toronto: Lester Publishing Limited, 1992.

Pitchfork, Graham. *Shot Down and on the Run: The RCAF and Commonwealth Aircrews Who Got Home from Behind Enemy Lines, 1940–1945*. Toronto: The Dundurn Group, 2003.

Roland, Charles G. *Long Night's Journey into Day: Prisoners of War in Hong Kong and Japan, 1941–1945*. Waterloo: Wilfrid Laurier University Press, 2001.

Stafford, David. *Secret Agent: The True Story of the Covert War Against Hitler*. New York: The Overlook Press, 2001.

Peter Conrad

Peter Conrad is a writer, editor and instructional designer in Edmonton, Alberta. He holds two bachelor degrees in education and history, as well as a master's in history from the University of Saskatchewan. When he's not hard at work, Peter enjoys spending time with his family and pursuing his other passion, art. He is the author of three young adult novels, three non-fiction books, one creative non-fiction book and numerous articles and short stories.

FOLKLORE PUBLISHING
Where History Comes Alive